A Word or Two

Christopher Andreae

PublishAmerica
Baltimore

First printing

ISBN: 1-4137-2743-3

PUBLISHED BY PUBLISHAMERICA, LLLP

www.publishamerica.com

Baltimore

Printed in the United States of America

To Morven for her remarkable tolerance.

Acknowledgments

All but one of the essays in this book were originally published in *The Christian Science Monitor*. I wish to thank all my editors on this paper and their assistants, past and present. Each essay in this selection has, however, been reedited. I have been immeasurably helped in this refining task by Jayne I. Hanlin. Almost all the essays have also been retitled for this compilation.

I would like to express specific gratitude to a number of other people who have helped me bring this entire project to a happy fulfillment by help and also by various sorts of encouragement. These kind people include Brian Andreae, Suzette Mitchell, Leigh Montgomery, Karen Zumbrunn, Maggie Thomas, and the editorial staff of PublishAmerica. And there are many others who have made me feel I have not just written these essays, put them in a bottle, and sent them out to sea never to be seen again: the people who have, over the years, generously opened the bottle and read my "word or two."

List of Contents

I.
Wordsmith

II.
Going to the Dogs

III.
And Other Animals

VII.
Children Seen and Heard

VIII.
Willingly to School?

IX.
Flower and Veg

X.
Protestations

XI.
Reading, Writing, Listening, and Looking

XII.
Making and Doing

I.
Wordsmith

Of Whiskers and Old Socks

In abstracted moments, one may ask, "How did I end up doing the job I am doing?" I do, anyway. Careers (although that word sounds a touch overstated) may not be what were intended at all.

When I was still (just) in secondary school, the people in charge had a bright idea. They thought they should have a Careers Master, someone to advise the boys on jobs. Strange as it may seem, this was a radical notion.

The new Careers Master hadn't the slightest clue about jobs. He had probably fallen into his own job by default. He'd been to university, and not having qualifications for anything in particular, he had taken up as a teacher because qualifications weren't needed.

You could do a year of "teacher training" after your degree—but only if you felt like it—and then you'd interview at some school or other, and they'd give you a job.

Anyway, in my last year or two at school, the Careers Master was tossed onto the shore. It was thought I might benefit from his services. So I went in to have a word with him.

I came out no wiser than when I went in. What was I any good at that might lead to a steady income? My chief accomplishments were painting (loved that), Ping-Pong (spent hours doing that), and acting (reveled in that), and I was not too bad at English, though no star pupil. The Careers Master must have looked at my record and shrugged helplessly.

In any event, I was fortunate enough to get into university—mainly on the strength of my older brother having gone to the college some years before. I'd also complimented the chaplain (one of my interviewers) on the felicity of his rock garden. Since I actually knew the difference between edelweiss and Gentiana acaulis, I think I impressed him.

University deferred worry about a job for four years. My hermetically sealed education continued for the duration.

Then I interviewed to become a teacher.

The world fell in! They gave the job to some other young man. Nothing to do with his aptitude or vocation. It was simply that he was good at rugby football. (I was not.)

In utter shame, I interviewed at another school, and for some inexplicable reason, they put me on their staff.

I think, in fact, they spotted a sucker-in-waiting. I was given all the low-achievers to teach, kids who had long ago given up any idea of education. This baptism of ashes lasted a year—a year too long.

I lasted another year at another school and really quite enjoyed it.

After that, I became a writer. Well, a sort-of feature journalist. An art critic. An essay writer. Not what you'd call a real career, of course, but at least I now found myself being paid (a little) for doing something for which my school career had actually, to some extent, prepared me—not that this preparation had been in any way deliberate. Indeed, it had nothing to do with the teachers at all.

I became employed as a writer on the strength of a few published essays. And the reason I took to the essay form had nothing to do with admiration for Joseph Addison or Dorothy Parker.

It stemmed directly from Bad Behavior.

The school I attended was not one of Britain's dyed-in-the-wool public schools, so the prefects were not allowed to beat the smaller boys like us. But they were allowed to dish out certain punishments designed to rid us, I imagine, of original sin.

It didn't work. Our sins went on being as original as ever. We did awful things … like talking when talking was forbidden. I still, unrepentantly, like doing that.

The usual punishment was writing an essay. Jogging around a playing field in the rain was another and not so much to my taste.

So, visualize the scene. Andreae has spoken when he shouldn't have. Worse still, he has been heard doing so.

Prefect: "That's it! Andreae! You will do 23 pages by lunchtime tomorrow … on … let me see …" A certain sadistic relish here as the prefect thinks of an impossible subject "On, yes—on whiskers. Any deviation from the topic and you'll do 23 more pages. Normal-size handwriting, please!"

Andreae (defiantly): "Whiskers? Easy. No problem! Three pages, was it?" But what people say and what they think are often different. I would actually be wondering how anyone could possibly write even half a page about whiskers. Or about raindrops on roses. Or warm woolen mittens. (These were a few of their favorite themes.)

But it's amazing how demand creates supply. Which is how I learned to write essays.

Not long ago, one of my editors (in a rare moment of foolhardy praise) said I could probably write an essay about anything—even old socks. It's true. I had already done so. Well, about socks, anyway.

But as I have now finally and publicly come clean about the shady origins of my essayism, I am forced to come to another conclusion. One with which I suspect many a real, truly career-driven writer will agree.

It is this: a writing career is at root one long punishment. Not at all what I intended as a lifetime thing. But has anyone out there got any suggestions for a good alternative?

2001

A Time to Exuberate Rumbustiously

Reticence and modesty best suit wordsmiths. I know this—falling, as I have unwittingly these many decades, under the dubious heading of "writer." We hacks have little to boast about by and large; silence would be agreeable gold for most of us (and our readers) were it not for the mundane need for bankable income. But, it is always an ultimate consolation to be conscious that no one is actually *forced* to read our verbalisms. It's a free world....

However, there are occasions when the call to exuberate, extravagate, and even indulge in overmuchness—indeed, to boast—is legitimate. Forgive me, but I feel this is one. "Some," an obscure 16th-century dramatist observed in the persona of one of his less likable characters, "have greatness thrust upon them." *C'est moi.*

Were it not for the eagle eyes of a longtime colleague, I would never, perhaps, have learned of my unexpected lurch into memorability: of my distinct, if tenuous, claim on posterity. He phoned from the United States (I live in Scotland) to let me know. It made my day.

The burden of his news: *I am in a dictionary!*

Some dictionaries support their definitions with quotations. To show a word in actual use, adds, I suppose, to the understanding of it. It's a policy of which the great Dr. Samuel Johnson, back in the mid-18th century, was an initial practitioner.

His compilation of English words in two volumes is arguably the mother of all dictionaries. Nor was he modest about his achievement. "I knew very well what I was undertaking—and very well how to do it—and have done it very well," was his assessment.

But words are fickle objects, coming and going with fashion, appearing sometimes only once, to fizzle out immediately like shy glowworms. Johnson mentions several he could find only a single use of; it is one of the engaging characteristics of his work that he thought some such words worthy of inclusion. Presumably, he just liked them.

A number of other words were so unfamiliar that he admitted ignorance of their meaning but still put them in his book. Then there were those words that were once newly born but had become rather old. In 1755, for instance, Johnson listed "knuff" (meaning "a lout") as "an old word." If it was old then, it seems to have become well and truly obsolete since.

What a pity! Johnson's quote is a verse sporting the phrase "country knuffs," and you instantly know the type he means: every small rural community has its congregation of them, loitering bored at some corner or leaning incogitatively over some bridge parapet. The world might well be duller without them. At school we used to call them "oicks" or "yobs," and I'm pleased to see the latest *Random House Webster's College Dictionary* (1991) mentions one of these (as "Brit. Slang"), if not the other. This inestimable dictionary is extremely hard to fault I find; but it doesn't include "knuff" … and it doesn't include "rumbustious." So according to this dictionary, it would no longer be in the least feasible to remark, as you drive through, say, a small English village, "I' faith, there be a rumbustious, nay, a coxcomical and noious cluster of ninnyhammers, noodles, and knuffs as ever I did see." (The rest is OK, but knuffs are snuffed.)

We, nowadays, have our own inventions, of course, like "herstory" for feminists with a past, and "advertorial" (which Johnson would have designated a "low cant word," I hope) for newspaper articles that appear independent but actually promote a sponsoring product. Low. Cant. Definitely.

Incidentally, Johnson has the following to say about "nowadays": "This word, though common and used by the best writers, is perhaps barbarous." It's still going strong, not yet a thing of yesteryear, and who with any sensitivity wouldn't prefer it to today's "this moment in time?" This ugly redundant cliché of ours is infinitely surpassed by Johnson's single-syllable word for the same thing: "nick."

But what concerns me at this nick is the word "rumbustious." A glorious, wonderful, notable, promotable, old giant of a word! Go on, say it! Roll it round your teeth! I hereby propose that the English-speaking world should make a concerted effort to keep alive the word "rumbustious." Listen to it! Its rumbling sound speaks eloquently of its right and might to survive. Please, my friends, do not let "rumbustious" become archaic or obsolete.

Pardon? You don't know what it means?

You can't find it in your dictionary?

Ah! What you need is a copy of *The American Heritage Dictionary of the*

English Language, Third Edition (coming out today, courtesy of Houghton Mifflin). This dictionary is without question or debate the finest, most complete, most subtle, most thoroughgoing, and most catagmatick (see Johnson) of dictionaries.

And in it, you will find, under "R," not far from "rumble seat" and "rummage sale," the word "rumbustious."

I quote:

rum.bus.tious … adj. Uncontrollably exuberant; unruly: *"Common to both his illustrations and his independent paintings … and lurking below their rumbustious surface, is a sympathy for the vulnerability of the ordinary human being" (Christopher Andreae).*

You see? Here is a magnificent arrangement of letters, a word worth fighting for, a word whose existence some lesser dictionaries do not even acknowledge (and some greater, too: surprisingly, Johnson himself did not, apparently, know of it). Yet the *American Heritage Dictionary* goes even further with this laudable, admirable, memorable word. It takes it into its extended forms as "adverb" and "noun":—rum.bus.tious.ly adv.—rum.bus.tious.ness n.

I've always liked this word. Nowadays I like it even more. But in the interests of absolute authenticity, I should perhaps confess to two salient things.

First, I haven't any recollection at all from the passage quoted, what artist's work I was writing about or when.

And second, I can never remember how to spell "rumbustious." I always have to look it up … in a dictionary.

1992

Danger: Booksellers at Work

Entering a secondhand bookseller's is an act of calculated temerity. Risky. Henry Ward Beecher knew this. "Where is human nature so weak as in the bookstore?" he wrote.

He was alluding to the way we fall irretrievably for a book we haven't the slightest wedge of shelf space for at home—a book that can be bought only by pawning one's sneakers. The urgency is compelling: buy it *now*, or you'll never see it again.

It is easy to bolster this with some poignant case history or other; for me, usually, it is the Picasso linocuts book. There, in the secondhand department of John Smith's in Glasgow, I held it in my very own hands. I purred louder with each turn of the page. But its exorbitant price I pondered at length. I put it tenderly back on the shelf behind the glass. Came back next day and looked again. Then I did a foolish thing.

I went to another rare bookdealer in town and mentioned, in passing, the price of the book at Smith's. "Oh," he said, "far too much. Don't buy it. I'll get you a copy at half the price."

He never has.

And someone else bought the book from his rival. I have not seen it anywhere since.

If this is not a good enough argument for immediately buying any book you want badly, then there is always Desiderius Erasmus who said: "When I get a little money, I buy books; and if any is left, I buy food and clothes." A sound bloke, Desid.

This particular risk, however, is not what I am talking about. Even more unsettling and possibly dangerous is what one might call the idiosyncrasy of booksellers. They are a peculiar people. Most of them charmingly admit this, but such self-knowledge serves only as self-encouragement.

I recall one in Cambridge, England. A notice on his door shouts: "I do not sell student texts. DON'T EVEN ASK!" The same man refuses to buy a French book of any kind, ever. "The French do not know how to make books" is his stern dictum.

When I told another bookman about this, he expressed outrage. "My goodness!" he exclaimed. "Mind you," he added, afterthoughtfully, "he's quite right."

Some booksellers have to be awakened out of deep sleep if you want one of their books.

Others—there is one in Edinburgh—are always so deep in conversation that you have to wait a long time for a gap—and even then they may accept your check, bag your book, and wave goodbye without noticing you at all. This book chap is one of my current favorites. On my second visit, I found him striding violently about between the piles of books, holding forth. Beside himself. Every syllable an indignant splutter. "They—come up here—from the south," he was exclaiming, "and because they are English, and because they went to public school, they treat us like peasant provincials who know nothing! How dare they? How *dare* they?"

He subsided finally. As quietly as I could, I remarked: "I wonder if you would in fact sell me a book—though I am both English and public-school educated."

He grinned broadly. "So am I," he said. Then: "Mind you, the public school I went to was somewhat 'different.'"

"Oh?"

"Manchester Grammar School."

"Ah," I chuckled knowingly, remembering an old friend who harked from the same establishment and was just as opinionated and vocal.

"And," he went on, "we were taught, above all, *tolerance*."

"Of course," I said.

He let me buy a couple of books.

Yesterday I bravely broached a bookshop new to me. The owner was white-haired and looked amiable. He seemed busy. I nosed among the stacks. There are various procedural rules you need to know in secondhanders. One is: never expect to find the book you are looking for.

As ever, the rule applied. The second rule is: don't tell the bookseller the name of the book you are looking for or ask if he has it. This can be a very unsafe procedure. The answer invariably will be "No," but this negative can take a number of forms, all discombobulating.

Here are some:

"I think I saw it once—but not for years." (Subtext: "And no-one else has either.")

"I am just sitting in for the owner. I don't know about his stock." (Subtext: "I am the owner, but I'm too tired to bother.")

"If you can't see it on the shelves, I do not have it." (Subtext: "What do you have eyes for?")

"I'm sorry, I am about to close." (Subtext: "I wish I'd closed before you came in.")

The book I wanted yesterday (I need it for my work—honest) was published in 1981 and is called—as I told the white-haired gentleman, thereby breaking Rule the Second—*Japonism*.

From a sanguine benevolence, he metamorphosed instantly into an opinionated hobbyhorse. "Never seen or heard of it! I don't like the sound of it at all. In fact, anything ending in '-ism' I do not like: monetar-ism, femin-ism, commun-ism, conservat-ism—think about it! What on earth is Japon-ism?" And he sat down again promptly, as if this ended the matter.

Afterward, I wished I had thought of adding to his list: "What about telev-ism?" Instead, I tried to explain Japonism. "Well, you know, it is the word for the influence of Japanese art on Western art after the opening up of Japan in 1853. Perhaps it sounds better in French—'Japonisme'?"

And that, for some reason, melted him. We chatted for about an hour. We aired our pet theories and opinions, setting the world to rights. We parted, eventually, friends. "Nice to meet you," he said. "Come again."

But before I left, this bookseller had told me two things that seem to sum up the paradoxical truculence and good humor of his kind.

"You know," he said, "the thing that really gets me is when people come in and say: 'Do you buy books?' I mean—what do they think I do? I usually say: 'Only the ones I can't steal.' And either they leave in shock or laugh. Do I buy books!"

The other thing was a story.

"I'll tell you the kind of happening typical of this shop. A young Malaysian woman came in with a friend. She looked round with this delight on her face. 'Oh!' she said. 'This is marvelous! It reminds me of a story I read as a child. About a bookshop, like this. Filled everywhere with books. And it had an old white-haired man in it. And he sold magic books!'

"So," he continued, "I immediately reached behind me for this book—and I said to her, 'You mean magic—like—this?' And I opened it up."

He took it down now and opened it up for me, too. Out of its pages sprang up, like a jack-in-the-box, an exotic, enchanted fairy-tale palace with onion turrets, set in a bright garden. And high above its vivid red roof flew a leaping horse and rider.

"She gasped and fell about laughing with surprise and wonder," he said. "It was the first time she had seen a pop-up book."

And that reminded me: I hadn't asked him if he had any pop-up books. As it happened, apart from "Japonism," I was also on the hunt for "Pop-up-ism."

"It is going to a good home," I assured him as he put it in a bag for me. (I need it for my work—honest.)

1996

In the Library, With a Book

Disney's *Beauty and the Beast* has an interesting underlying theme. The heroine, Belle, is a bookworm. In the never-never-land castle, as its enchanted inhabitants are not slow to realize, there is one room above all that would appeal to this spirited young lass. When the Beast wants to be kind to her (having already heroically saved her from a pack of wolves), he takes her to this room and just gives it to her, as a present.

It is the library.

But what a library! A gigantic, hyperbolic, amazing fantasy that has in it billions more books than imagination can compass, tiers upon tiers of shelves crammed to the gills, and galleries rising above galleries, climbing endlessly up into incalculable heights with—of course—*ladders* for accessibility. The Disney studio never could do anything by halves, and the 1990s are no exception. This is meant to be the *ultimate* in private libraries.

The assumption is that Belle will find in this mind-boggling room everything her literary heart could desire. It is a sign that, despite his rather unpromising appearance, Beast is sensitive to the finer aspects of home life. In this he contrasts markedly with the vain and macho suitor in the village who is determined to have Belle for a wife by fair means or foul, mostly foul.

His brand of crassness is chiefly demonstrated by a hatred for books. Belle should stop stuffing her head with stories and be his good little undistracted and mindless spouse. He treads the book she is reading firmly into a puddle to make his point. So books and the traditional room afforded them become crucial symbols in this modernly rejigged folk tale.

It's a nice touch.

Libraries in our time are most frequently public. Reasons of space and cost alone militate against the library in the home being a commonplace. Kitchens, bathrooms, even TV rooms, seem established enough. However, the library, though reaching its peak in houses of the wealthy or scholarly in the 18th and 19th centuries, has never really been an absolute essential in the home.

Even at its most popular, when it was certainly a status symbol to own and display books (the 20th-century coffee table book remains as our attenuated version of this harmless vanity), the library in the home still had a rather undecided character.

In the 18th century, what had been a room with a fairly exclusive function for perhaps a century, had in some cases evolved into a kind of family room. A William Hogarth portrait of the Cholmondeley family (1732) presents them all—children and dog, too—in the library. Indeed, the kids are mucking about with the books. In other large houses, the library as pictured by artists or, later, by photographers, has become quite definitively the living room. The walls may be lined with bookcases, but the central space is filled with capacious and comfortable furniture. The wonderful habit of reading aloud to the assembled family for an evening—television has done in that idea forever—may have been a factor in bringing living room and library together in this way. In other houses, the billiard table somehow found its way into the library. So, then, which was it primarily, a games room or a reading place?

It is interesting that in the Disney fantasy, the library is thought to be just the place for a young lady. If the presumed period is sort of medieval, this is a remarkably inaccurate notion. Not only most women, but also most men, were illiterate, even among the wealthy classes. The ecclesiasts were literate and had their libraries. But not the gentry or aristocracy. One early 16th-century English gentleman is said to have observed: "I'd rather that my son should hang than study letters. For it becomes the son of a gentleman to blow the horn nicely, to hunt skillfully and elegantly, to carry and train a hawk. But the study of letters should be left to the sons of rustics."

Until well into the 17th century, there was simply no call for a separate room for books in the majority of homes. Even some of the wealthiest and most cultured still had very few volumes of their own and kept them in a chest, or perhaps in some small room adjoining the bedroom or family chapel.

When libraries started to become a standard expectation of properly equipped houses, they were still not large, containing usually no more than a few hundred books. It became a matter of hospitality that a friend or visitor would be given free access to the library; the books were collected to be shared.

But such generosity was counterbalanced, in some cases, by the distinctly fostered idea that the library was a place of escape, particularly for the man of the house. This may have been partly because "library" and "study" were not always clearly separated, and the master's study was quite certainly his domain.

In Jane Austen's *Pride and Prejudice* (first published 1813), the father of the five eligible Bennet girls seeks quiet and solace in the reading of books, or, in time of greatest need, by simply disappearing into his library. Unfortunately for him, though, the door is not locked against the importunities of his troublesome wife, who invades his sanctum and demands that he insist his daughter Elizabeth accept the marriage proposal of Mr. Collins.

Unmoved among his books, he explains steadily to his favorite daughter her predicament: if she does not accept Mr. Collins, she will fatally alienate her mother, but if she does accept him, she will lose the love of her father. She must decide. The implication, I believe, is that the place in the home to be Solomon-wise and witty is the library.

At another moment in the same wonderful book, Austen makes humor out of the notion of a particular room demanding particular kinds of talk and thought; as they dance and make awkward conversation, Elizabeth banteringly tells Darcy (for whom she is destined): "No—I cannot talk of books in a ballroom; my head is always full of something else." The fact seems to be that a library as part of the home seems to be as varied in concept as that home's particular owners, apart from the basic idea that it is the place where books are kept when there are sufficient numbers of them to demand attention. So in one Victorian house—in the English county of Northumberland—what is called the library has in it several low shelves along the walls, but a host of china and ornaments as well, and pre-Raphaelite paintings taking up all of the upper half of the walls. Books have their place, but they hardly predominate. The late 17th century library in Ham House, Surrey, on the other hand, had two rooms for books, the "library" and the "library closet." Though not enormous, they were nevertheless filled with shelving. They were placed somewhere between the private and the more public parts of the house, accessible to both.

In one grand late 19th-century house, one of the children later recorded that it was the library into which visiting prime ministers were ushered.

Literati, naturally, have their own attitudes toward libraries. Thomas de Quincey, 19th-century essayist, for example, dreamt of an ideal library (which was apparently a long way from his own chaotically messy setup). He called on an imaginary painter to "paint" it for him: "Paint me, then, a room seventeen feet by twelve…. Make it populous with books … a good fire and furniture plain and modest, befitting the unpretending cottage of a scholar.

And near the fire, paint me a tea-table...." James Henry Leigh Hunt, another essayist and book lover, figured out an essential difference between the library as a sizeable (but never large enough) space where books are stored and the room where books are most enjoyably read. Some people think that room is the bedroom, or even, for uninterruptible solitude, the bathroom. But Leigh Hunt proposed a "small, snug" study. There, he said, "I entrench myself in my books equally against sorrow and the weather."

Where the library was in a house may not have been clearly delineated because it was capable of being anything from a selfish indulgence to a utilitarian and needful reference to a room of considerable sociableness and sharing.

There are cases where the wealthy house owners deliberately made their libraries accessible to their upper servants and where children were encouraged to develop an early delight in books. Others were no-go areas. Some owners of private libraries were outgoing to a fault, lending and borrowing books being part of their pleasure. Others are said to have never parted with a book during their lifetimes.

"Borrowed" books can be a bone of contention between collectors or simply a matter of forgetfulness, sometimes for a decade or two. Samuel Pepys, a 17th-century English diarist, is known to have borrowed more books from his friend John Evelyn than Evelyn borrowed from him. Some of Evelyn's books have stayed permanently, I believe, in Pepys' library of 3,000 volumes, which is now housed in perpetuity at Magdalene College, Cambridge.

Pepys was a more than enthusiastic owner of a private library par excellence; he loved the subjects of his books, but he also just plain loved books. "My delight is in the neatness of everything," he said. He loved bindings. In one of his rearrangements of his library, he organized them in order of size! But for appearance he had little wooden plinths disguised with gilt leather made so that they would all look the same height on the shelves. He also had a library stepladder—a sure sign that the library is truly worthy of its title and is not just some room where the books have all washed up. Pepys was a short man and needed his steps. But tall book collectors need them, too, if their upper shelves are higher than eight feet up. Some book collectors buy books for their private libraries one or two at a time. But others, J. Pierpoint Morgan, for instance, also bought whole libraries. He rapidly had space problems in the cluttered basement room of his Madison Avenue house. So, at vast expense, a new building next door was built, connected by an underground passage.

Historian Edward Gibbon was one of those who made himself a library for sound scholarly reasons. His nearly 7,000 volumes were what he needed to write his magnum opus, *History of the Decline and Fall of the Roman Empire.* He claimed (I think rather prissily) he was not "conscious of ever having bought a book from a motive of ostentation."

It has been said more than once that a sure way to poverty is to collect books. To collect books—and have a private library for them—does require plenty of money. While Gibbon's boast is impressive, no less impressive is the contribution to the world made by some writers who have been financial light years away from having a library.

Today you don't need one, with all the lending and reference libraries so easily usable. Computer buffs wildly predict the disappearance of books.

However, bookshops become larger and larger, and the thirst for book ownership evidently increases rather than abates. The only question is: where in a modern house are they all kept?

1992

II.
Going to the Dogs

Spot, Domino and the Emmas

It isn't too hard to spot a Dalmatian.

For a start, there's the way they rush up and greet you—you, their long lost friend—as soon as they know you are an authentic visitor in their domain. No matter that they've never met you before. You are made to feel overwhelmingly at home, greeted and fêted.

Then there's the way they wash you. They start with your hands, but soon move on with disarming affection to your chin, your nose, stretching their elegant necks upward like canine swans, tongue busy with kind attentions. You might as well be one of their puppies. There's no escape from such a degree of maternal cleanup. You must endure. To do otherwise would be to flout Dalmatian etiquette.

Then there's the concentrated way they eye the piece of cake in your hand. You thought it was meant entirely for you? The eyes inform otherwise. Dalmatians' eyes are knowing and keen—super-keen when there's cake. But they also suggest vulnerability. They say: "You realize, don't you, that we Dalmatians are sensitive flowers and can be easily dismayed?" This is a blatant lie—a ruse—because, at the same time, these eyes are just *daring* you to ignore their importunity. It is a form of exquisitely refined and complex emotional blackmail. It means: "If you don't give me at least a third of that delectable-looking slice of raspberry-and-cream sponge, don't imagine that I will withdraw the extreme and impartial affection I bear you; I won't. Never fear, you will still be the human I love better than any other in the entire cosmos.

"Bu-ut, you know, IF you should just happen, with what I know is your characteristic generosity, to feel like sharing with your devoted servant a little bit of that, oh dear, much-too-rapidly diminishing piece of cake, then I promise to double, perhaps even t-r-e-b-l-e the intensity of my adoration for you. Really, even a tiny crumb will suffice.... M-m-m, *gulp*, thanks, any more?"

Then there is the way they sit on you. This is one of their more enchanting and weighty traits. As with cake, so with sofas or armchairs: these are things for sharing. Dog beds are all right so far as they go, but human accommodation is so much more satisfactory and friendly. The best seats of all, though, are human laps. Laps are the tops—laptops.

Eleanor Frankling, in her authoritative, much reprinted and revised book, *The Dalmatian*, writes about this characteristic while discussing the various depictions of Dalmatians in art. She refers to a late 17th-century painting called *Hunting Dogs and Their Attendants*. In the foreground of this exuberant painting are two Dalmatians. One of them is in "I-am-getting-quickly-on-your-lap" mode. The boy who is being climbed upon is not much larger than the dog. But size has little to do with it. Judgment of appropriate scale seems not to be a strong point when it comes to lap-climbing. Frankling says the dog in the painting has "a typical Dalmatian attitude … for many Dalmatians believe themselves to be lap dogs, and get as much of their anatomy as possible onto the knees of their friends."

And then their spots. Didn't I mention them? They come in black, but also in brown, or liver as it is known. And every Dalmatian, naturally, has at least a hundred and one of them. They carry them proudly. They carry *themselves* proudly, these spotty dogs.

In the book that has done more to popularize Dalmatians and their spots than any other (with a little additional help from Walt Disney), author Dodie Smith describes her heroes, Pongo and Missis, as they go for a walk with their humans, Mr. and Mrs. Dearly, to celebrate the news that Missis is soon to produce puppies. The book is, of course, *The Hundred and One Dalmatians*.

Smith writes: "The Dearlys led the way.... Then came the Pongos, looking noble; they could both have become champions if Mr. Dearly had not felt that dog shows would bore them—and him. They had splendid heads, fine shoulders, strong legs, and straight tails. The spots on their bodies were jet-black and mostly the size of a two-shilling piece; they had smaller spots on their heads, legs, and tails. Their noses and eye-rims were black.... They walked side by side with great dignity, only putting the Dearlys on the leash to lead them over crossings."

Who says they don't like being on show?

I myself once had a live-in Dalmatian for a year or so. Her owners were abroad. While she was with me, in spite of her undoubted superiority and urban manners, she learned to be "just a country dog." But I think she secretly held on to a conviction of superiority all the same. Being myself by nature (and breeding?) a mutt-man, I admit to finding the dedication of Dal fanciers (as I believe they call themselves) to the perfect specimen half admirable and half funny. I admire it as I admire any idealism. But by the same token, an obsessive concern for "scissor bite" or "elastic pads"—not to mention "fine texture" in ears and a "moderate amount of stop" in the head and skull, and no "wrinkle"—does have its absurd side. This is especially so when you consider how the humans demanding such physical perfection can themselves be all shapes and sizes. We do to the canine species what we would—or should—resist to the death if it were to be applied, by geneticists in the pay of a tyrant, to humans.

Kennel names for dogs are an endless source of amusement, belonging to a fantasy world. Now and then one comes across Dalmatian names that seem perfectly apt—"Snow Leopard" seems a good one, poetic and unpretentious. More show-doggish is "Sugarfrost Buttons and Bows." But I think my favorite—and I promise I didn't make this name up—is "Olbero Organized Confusion." That's a Dalmatian all right.

Dalmatians have had a historical role. They were "carriage dogs." Pictures show them prancing along by the horse-drawn carriages of their aristocratic owners. Two wood-engraved tail pieces by the great 18th-century English engraver and naturalist Thomas Bewick depict such spotted dogs, as does one of his main illustrations, and it is in this book, *History of Quadrupeds,* that the first firm insistence on the name "Dalmatian" appears in print. It says "The Dalmatian, or coach dog ... is very common in this country at present; and is frequently kept in genteel houses, as an elegant attendant on a carriage." The Dalmatian was, in fact, frequently kept with the horses, in the stables. Just as individual sheep have been known to become inseparable friends with horses, so have the dogs.

A friend of mine who owns a delightful Dalmatian (named Emma) remembers, when she lived in Canada as a young girl, that her first-known Dalmatians, Spot and Domino, were always around the stables. And being carriage dogs led them to another association. Beverley Pisano, in her 1990 book *Dalmatians* writes: "What could have been more natural than for the firemen to adopt the Dalmatian as their mascot in the days of the horse-drawn fire engines?" And she claims, "There is hardly a firehouse that doesn't have the coach dog as its pet and companion for the men."

Most Dalmatians today, however, are surely just pets. I asked Emma's owner why she favors the breed. "Oh!" she exclaimed, ecstasy suffusing her voice. "Whenever I'm driving along in the car, and I see a Dalmatian, I just go all wobbly!" What this does to her driving I didn't like to inquire. But she then tried to explain further: "They have wonderful carriage. And a wonderful smile. And happy tails."

Not all Dalmatians wag their tails as readily as her Emma does. She just can't stop. Even when having her claws clipped, which she dislikes so intensely that it takes two people to stop her bolting, her tail still wags. Emma's Dalmatian predecessor (also named Emma) was probably more typical of the "courtesy" that some say is a Dalmatian trait. She could be a little standoffish until she got to know you. But today's Emma "loves everyone."

I can vouch for it. Visiting Emma's house one day, I made the mistake of wearing a navy blue woolen sweater. Emma, in character, sat all over me for much of our visit. It took *three weeks* of patient work before I had removed, from the interstices of every remote reach of every last nook, cranny, and cross-stitch of that sweater, all of the several billion short white hairs that had insinuated themselves inextricably therein like minuscule porcupine quills.

"It's their only fault," admits Emma's owner. "They do shed all the time."

Quite. I suppose one should be grateful they only seem to shed their white hairs—and not their black spots.

1993

The Sleeping-Dog Factor

The dog very clearly had something to do with it. There, on a recent front page of one of the "heavies" (as the newsagents like to dub the two or three British newspapers that require a modicum of literacy from their clientele), was a photograph of "Philip Pennington, a 33-year-old shepherd from Moulton, Northamptonshire, at a London press conference to celebrate his Open University Bachelor of Arts degree. He is with his collie, Tess."

Indeed he is. Tess is gazing at her thoroughly bearded, smiling, crook-carrying master as though waiting for nothing more than a wink-signal to go and round up the photographers. Hers is a look of total devotion, of unquestioning obedience—and of canine purpose. In a word, this dog is bachelor-of-arts material.

But of course, it was the shepherd, and not the collie, who had just gained a degree, by what must surely be the most laborious and admirable of methods—that of the correspondence course. But does her boss fully realize, I wonder, the extent and nature of Tess's contribution?

One doesn't need to talk with this stalwart man of the hills and dales of Northamptonshire to know for a certain fact that on the endless evenings he spent poring over the awkward niceties of *The Role of Houseflies in the Novels of William Golding* or *The Evidence of Imperialist Ambition in the Style of Jackson Pollock's Work of the Middle Period* (the photo caption does not mention specifically the subject of his degree), his dog was sound asleep at his feet—even, possibly, draped over his feet—dreaming of this, that, and the other.

She was *asleep*; that's the point. She wasn't awake and champing. She wasn't sitting bolt upright and staring at him. She wasn't getting up, turning round, sighing loudly, and flopping down again. She wasn't whining or standing disconsolately with nose pressed hard against the door. She wasn't placing her head firmly on his knee and wagging her other end. She wasn't, in a nutshell, demanding a walk.

There seems little doubt that in his excellent dog's disinclination to go for walks, lies, in considerable measure, the secret of his success degree-wise. The sleeping-dog factor is an important part of much academic brilliance. This can be deduced by simple reversal: how many theses remain incomplete, how many books still wait to be read or written, how many researches lie unresearched because the dog must go out?

Mr. Pennington can indeed be grateful. His Tess's doziness is the direct result of the joint calling of this dog and her shepherd. She gets automatically and overwhelmingly exercised, and, come the evening, she, like her master, wants a change. She is only too happy to chase dreams instead of sheep.

And now let us consider our new arrival, our own recently adopted dog, named (after much consideration) "Wolf." My wife and I selected him with the utmost care at that Dickensian institution in Glasgow, the "Dog and Cat Home," because his quiet, unmoving, stay-at-home reserve greatly impressed us; not that either of us is thinking of taking a correspondence course—but just on the principle that what is good for studious shepherds is likely not to be all that bad for the rest of us.

"Wolf" sat with his back pressed against the cage. He was stationary except for his head, which he turned away and then again turned away. Reticence and placidity were written all over him. There was no way he was going to leap up and down, dance, and bark like all the other silly dogs in the place, all so hyper-anxious to be out and about, yelling and screaming. Here, we felt certain, was our ideal—a mature, dignified, patient dog, happy to sit and think a lot, or even just to sit.

We were wrong, naturally. Wolf, it turns out, is keenly peripatetic. Each day, in fact, he reveals a fresh facet of his enthusiasm for *the walk*. The only thing wrong with any walk in his eyes is that it comes to an end. Home is *OK*, but away is far better.

I am even beginning to wonder if we haven't named him too suggestively—having since discovered that wolves are noted for speed of travel and an inexhaustible capacity to cover great distances—30 to 40 kilometers—in a mere night. Our "Wolf" breasts the wind with a not dissimilar determination and is all too adept at disappearing beyond horizons.

I am aware that the Dog Walk is a practice that may well seem absurd to those of other cultural heritages. But here in Britain the general routine—if not the positive and decent duty—of dog-owners is that they accompany their dogs on the run. (Cats are different for some reason.) To shove a dog out the back door and let him exercise himself is considered churlish, if not downright unkind. To emphasize the necessity of this national quirk, writers of dog manuals in Britain make much ado of *the walk*. Recently, indeed, one Emma De'ath, writing in my wife's latest issue of *Harpers&Queen,* goes so far as to dictate the correct duration of walks for different breeds.

German shepherds, she commands, shall be given two daily walks of 40 minutes. Labradors must have one good walk a day of 60 minutes (three fields). Rough collies need a full 80 minutes, and Irish setters, whose "exuberance and high spirits should not be deprived of wide-open spaces," should get no less. (Chihuahuas, Yorkshire terriers, and King Charles spaniels, on the other hand, are of the "two-twenty-minute-walks-per-day" class.)

Emma De'ath prints no figures for dogs of indeterminate or mixed parentage, so I suppose we mongrel-owners have to work it out for ourselves. Our own eager character looks like a mixture of German shepherd and rough collie, with a patch of golden Labrador on the back somewhere, and has a red-setterish élan and husky-like sticking-power to his exuberance and high spirits. He is also a mottled pink, black, and white round the chops, faintly hinting at Dalmatian input—a breed famous for running all day behind horse-drawn carriages.

In brief, he is an 80-minuter throughout and betrays not the faintest trace of Chihuahua, not the slightest fondness for sleep, and not even the most latent or subterranean inkling of an interest in Higher Education.

1984

It's a Bird! It's a Plane! It's a Dog!

This dog of ours has an ambition: to *fly*. If we had been initially perceptive, I suppose, we might have guessed as much.

Those ears of Wolf's, though they don't actually stick out sideways like wings, do, in the Alert Position, have something aeronautical about them. They look as though they might lift a body free of gravitational requirements, given a chance.

And that tail. Though to the uninformed it might suggest little more than a spring-like appendage of notable curvilinearity, it does have a hint of fin about it, now I give the matter thought. Streamlined to a degree, it might grace an eccentric flying machine.

He fell down the stairs into the kitchen the other morning—a whole flight of stairs. But the occurrence was, essentially, more acrobatic than aerodynamic. The fact is, he wasn't entirely expecting it. It came about because he happened to be lying in the I've-Been-Forgotten-About-Once-Again Position on the landing, and my pre-breakfast approach prompted him to display such an abandonment of exaggerated canine delight, rolling over on his back, that he miscalculated things, and down he went.

Neither he nor his pride was in the least shaken (and he is unusual among dogs in my experience for having very little pride to stand in the way of enjoying life). He bumped in a relaxed fashion on his spine down ten of the steps and took the last three on a rather approximate arrangement of feet. I think he may simply have thought it quite a novel and conveniently speedy manner of arriving at his food bowl.

But no, that isn't the kind of flight he is out for. Besides, this ambition doesn't really show up indoors.

Like most of us—though in varying degrees no doubt—this dog has a private face and a public face. He is almost two dogs, indoor dog and outdoor dog.

Affection and all its attendant performances, such as sitting on feet, nibbling feet, getting under feet, and so forth are in-house affairs. But the open air transforms him. Immediately there is business to attend to. No longer is it necessary to be nice to one's human beings. Much more significant events are afoot. They can whistle as much as they like and cajole and order and plead, but I, Public Dog No.1, have no time now for such minor noises. I—for instance—see a cat!

Now the odd thing about cats is that, again, Wolf's private and public attitudes are poles apart. In the house, the dog is perfectly content to let the house cat snuggle comfortably into his fur for many a dozing hour on end. But a cat seen along the road or on a front doorstep or watching for mice in the long grass! That cat is Big Game.

And around here, there are hundreds of cats, all of them terrorized to their whiskers' ends by this great thug of a mongrel who keeps thundering threateningly across their territory. They run (cats never learn), and the dog follows spontaneously, a furious, tearing, crazy thing with only one apparent notion: Catch! Catch! CATCH!

Has he ever caught a cat? Of course not. He'd be flabbergasted if he did. What would he do with it? Fortunately, however, this age-old arrangement, this habit, of cats and dogs ends differently. Either the cat proves an escape artist and vanishes completely, leaving the dog in a state of frenetic bafflement. Or—as happens here frequently—the cat scatters itself erratically up a tree and, back humped, fur puffed, nostrils twitching, and eyes rounded, balances on the highest branch available.

It is at this point precisely that the dog's ambition to fly shows itself. He seems to have deep resources of optimism on the subject. He seems utterly convinced that if he only runs fast enough at the tree trunk and throws himself into the air high enough, he will sprout wings, and, suddenly floating effortlessly on the air currents, he will approach the maddeningly complacent feline up there as a triumphant dog-bird, master of a new dimension, Flying Lord of the Cats. He leaps and yells and yells and leaps, high jumper extraordinary. But then he always falls back to earth with a thud. "Oh where, oh where, are my wings?" he screams.

He's studying the problem. When we go down into the long grass, and there are no cats in the offing, he studies the birds. He's not fussy as to species. Magpies will do as well as redstarts; crows are good because they're slow; fieldfares and sparrows twittering among the bog sedge are also fine: they all, after all, *know* how to fly.

He studies them by rushing at them. This makes them demonstrate for his personal observation the principles of the skill. They flap away a few feet above his head, not really startled, because they seem to know intuitively that, since the world began, a flying dog has not often been come across. He runs along under them, ears in Alert Position, tail cocked, head straining upward, urging liftoff, gasping to grasp its mechanics.

To date, his experiments are still on the drawing board of his dreams. His technology does not seem equal to his vision. But he never gives up—aware, no doubt, that this sort of attitude springs eternal.

We encourage him, naturally. If he learns, maybe his humans will get the trick of it, too. And then the cats better watch out.

1984

Dodge the Puppy, Olé

There are those, I suppose, who espouse the notion of unpredictability being the spice of life.

As for me, a second career as a matador was not specifically on my agenda. For a start, I do not possess a suitable cloak. No cloak at all, as it happens.

And there are other things I do not have that make (presumably) a matador's life a happy one: aggravating pokey things and so forth—you know, a spangly jacket-thing like colored sugar and trousers so sleek and tight-fitting that they would be just the thing for a waiter in an Italian bistro. Oh, and a silly moustache. These things I have not. And I am glad.

But I—no, I mean, we—do have a puppy. This event (and *event* is exactly the right word) was not actually on the agenda for me and my wife either, but there it is.

If you haven't had a puppy for a while, you forget what a puppy is like. Weather-words are helpful—boisterous, blustery—but finally they are not strong enough. We are talking whirlwind, tornado, big bang theory.

She is called Muff. Please don't ask me why. The naming of dogs is an impossible matter, and for two days she had no name of any sort. Neither of us is keen on animal names borrowed from humankind, like Belinda or Muriel. And funny names sound good for a moment, but are not entirely practical.

I've always felt "Loose-End" a perfect dog name, but I have doubts about yelling it across an open and public space in the event of some canine misdemeanor. While we cogitated, someone told me of a dog belonging to a friend of her daughter. He was named Burglar (conceptually an altogether reasonable name). But when said daughter was looking after Burglar one time, and he ran to the far side of the local park, and she tried to summon him by name—instead of the dog returning instantly, two puffing off-duty policemen materialized. They had been jogging and had heard her cries for help.

41

Unlike her wolfish predecessor, this new recipient of our affections and food is an inveterate stick-chaser. In fact, she is a chaser, pure and simple. Wolf chased cats. But Muff chases anything that moves or can be moved: breeze-wafted almond blossom petals, jogging constables, feathers, leaves, balls, bicycles, rubber rings, and all dogs of any sort whatsoever.

But, above all, sticks.

There are special parts of the park where the mown grass stretches out wide and long, and these are now Muff-playgrounds where sticks can be thrown in any direction, and, by demand, continuously forever.

It is the running that most appeals, not the sticks as such. Nothing pleases her more than to fly like an arrow 100 feet one way, grab the twirling stick, and then notice that I have another stick that I am planning to throw 100 feet the other way. She crouches for a split second in anticipation, and then— *swoosh!*—she charges straight ahead and past us like a hounded deer, certain that by the time she arrives at her destination, so will the airborne stick. But often enough, I propel one stick as best I can and then for love or money cannot find another in time for the rebound. Muff spots this failing and decides she had better bring back to me the stick she has just retrieved. Now I assume Labradors and spaniels (and whatever other breeds are retrievers by nature) understand that to bring a stick back to one's humans means literally running with it to them.

But Muff, who has no breed to name, does not see much point in this. When she runs back with a stick, she *accelerates* as she approaches and then—doesn't stop. She simply throws herself—dog leapant, stick in mouth—straight at you. It's an exhilarated, joie-de-vivre kind of business, but to be frank, it is a trifle destabilizing.

The first time it happened, from behind, I was shifted from vertical to horizontal without the passage of time being in the least involved. Since, on consideration, I have concluded that spontaneous recumbency is not my preferred way of going for a walk in a park with a dog on a nice sunny spring day, I am now much more prepared for such impending doom when it threatens.

It is even more sublimely terrifying if the retrieved stick, dancing ominously between her teeth like horns, happens to be one of her favorite tree trunks, *elephantinely* gigantic and massively weighty. (Incidentally, can anyone tell me whether all puppies lack a sense of proportion? Muff seems to feel that an ancient oak bole is just as suitable a plaything as the merest leaf stem.)

So I have found it essential to develop certain side-stepping tactics. They are almost balletic in their grace and suave beauty. They have to be at the very last minute. If Muff spots them too soon, she changes direction like a heat-seeking missile in order to be right on target.

At the crucial, make-or-break instant, in the flick of an eyelid, with a resplendent swish and a neatly calculated twist of the hip and thigh, my teeth flashing with sudden dazzlement in the fierce noon sunlight and a crowd-rousing suggestion of equine arrogance palpitating my fine nostrils, I take the thundering foe utterly by surprise. My extravagant evasion is, in a word, superb—a masterstroke of improvisational deftness.

The dog, missing her target completely, charges forward with dolphinlike abandon, wondering what on earth has happened to her brakes. And my life is saved once again. In short, I have become a matador.

You think I exaggerate?

1997

III.
And Other Animals

Unqualified Cat

As everyone knows, when it comes to the art of cool presumption, few creatures are as practiced as cats.

They take you entirely for granted, expect to be fed on demand, would rather starve than ingest inferior brands of cat food, leap without a by-your-leave onto furniture or laps in the clear consciousness that such things are provided for their sole use.

Cats are aesthetes. Their tastes aren't basic or obvious; they are cultivated and esoteric. Why a cat purrs or doesn't purr in any given situation is one of those age-old, dark enigmas. It isn't some involuntarily triggered response; oh no—it involves consideration. It involves lengthy meditation. A purr (and purrs come in varying degrees of intensity) is a value judgment. It shrewdly answers the inward query: "Is this stroking (holding, talking, feeding, etc.) actually worthy of acknowledgment?" It is rare for a purr to reach beyond the stage of a *qualified* approval.

What other creature is so breathtakingly skilled in making dependence look like independence? What other creature (like royalty conferring a title) bestows a well-deserved affection on you as though it were the greatest honor? Certainly cats are presumptuous, and what's worse, they are stinting in their gratefulness. And yet—just occasionally—there emerges from this unpredictable species some delightful (and delighted) spirit, some exception to feline rule.

Such as my ginger cat. A friend describes him as "everything a cat should be" or, in other words, everything a cat usually isn't. For a start, he, ginger cat, almost never expresses annoyance. He overspills with the most extraordinary thankfulness. Glance at him, and he purrs. Touch him, and he rolls over instantly on his back—it doesn't matter where, in the middle of a field, on a bed, on the front doorstep. He can be curled secure in an embryonic sleep, but he instantly throws all four arms widely in the air, issues small noises of utter contentment, and as you inevitably stroke him, he smiles. As Lewis Carroll knew, there is something indelible about a cat's smile, but this cat never disappears leaving his smile behind. He sticks around wherever his smile happens to be. He doesn't want to miss one moment of happiness.

Of course it is true that, like many good cat-human relationships, mine with this cat started out as cheek and nerve. At that time, he was as wild as he is now tame. He melodramatically haunted the farmhouse and buildings for some six months while I, in no way planning to add a second cat to my collection, pretended to ignore his somewhat heavy-footed presence.

Not that I could approach him in any case. If he saw me coming, he charged for cover in abject fright.

I don't believe his cheek was intentional—rather more instinctual. He is no calculating cat. But the fact is that one summer day a momentarily open kitchen door and some meat left carelessly on the table was too much of an invitation. The skulking ginger cat from the wild made his first daredevil break-in.

By what process that untame animal was transformed into the glorious object of routine domesticity is a story in itself. But one thing is certain: it was, however misguidedly, human kindness (with a little bit of milk) that made the first approach. That cat took nothing for granted. But when he discovered that the permanent (and transient) people in the house were generous enough to put out food for him, and then, very tentatively, to try to touch him, a sudden revelation occurred. "*This*," announced some deep-seated feline voice, "is the *life*."

Is it true that only those who have been deprived can know real gratitude? Surely not, but all the same I do feel the ginger cat has never quite forgotten what it is to be *without*, and this is why he never ceases to marvel at the delights of being *with*.

If you think a cat can't marvel, meet this one. It is as if the fondness of people came as an astounding bolt from the blue, as something that the sweetest of dreams could hardly concoct. He was taken by complete surprise and has never forgotten it. And he can't be loved too much.

His "capacity receiveth as the sea." Not for him the unfelicitous trait of being unable to take too much attention; not for him the sudden bite and claw and furious oscillation of the tail when the strain of being loved gets too great. This round cat is the epitome of endless welcome, entirely tolerant. Pick him up, put him down, let him in, throw him out, feed him, refuse him food—all is fine with him.

What cat in the world purrs like a motorbike when you push him through the back door into a snowstorm in December? This one does. Gratitude altogether overwhelms circumstance. Is such a complete lack of criticism, such an abandonment of judgment in favor of sheer, inexhaustible appreciativeness, perhaps just a mite stupid? Well ... yes ... maybe just a *mite* stupid.

I shall have to admit that intellectual acuity might possibly be more potential than evident in this ginger cat—just as physical nimbleness (natural to most cats) is not his strongest point. He thunders, herdlike, across a room or a field to greet you, or jumps like a hundredweight of potatoes off a table. His brand of tenderness is definite, bold, unremitting, unsubtle, heavy, and meant. It is not delicate. But, good heavens, this solid mass of warmth and daftness certainly makes you feel as though you *matter*.

1980

The Mouse Question

Glasgow. Tea time. The dog has sighted a bee. His ears are at alert. The bee is on the wrong side of the window at the bottom of the stairs.

The dog shifts spontaneously into murder mode. Now (though normally sweet-natured) he is a self-hired hit dog, a bee assassin. He is bigger than the bee, as mountains are to molehills. But the truth is that his implacable hatred of bees stems from cowardice and terror. He buffaloes himself at the window.

Heroically, I step in and save the bee. Meanwhile my wife's school-ma'am voice thunders from the table: "Wolf!" it yells, "Stop that! You wee, sleekit, cow'rin', tim'rous beastie, och, what a panic's in thy breastie!" The dog looks hurt for a second and then sits aloofly on the stairs as if nothing has occurred. The thing is, you can never be entirely sure what expressive phrase a Scottish person is going to come out with next—or at least that's my experience, being English but with this close-at-hand above-the-border connection.

My wife seems to have an inborn fund of Scottish expressions, osmosed, I suspect, at her mother's knee. I know I haven't heard them all yet, because every twelve months or so, a new one suddenly surfaces like a forgotten bubble from the ocean floor. "What does that mean?" I ask, amazed. And she, obligingly, dredges her folk-memory and translates for the resident foreigner.

Not that I am entirely the alien I might appear to be. I actually had a Scottish grandmother. I find it helpful at home to mention this fact as an aside in moments of underdogness, though I'm not sure I'm altogether believed. The problem is that although my grandmother's name was unquestionably "Burn"—surely Scottish—I never met the lady or learned anything at all about her, so I can't be totally convincing about her national allegiances.

All of which has little to do with "the mouse question." Well, no, perhaps, after all, it *does* have something to do with it. My granny was a singular Burn, but much more common is the pluralized version—which brings me to the

50

great national poet, Robert Burns.

Burns is as likely as anyone to be the source of suddenly surfacing Scottishisms or spontaneous bursts of Scottish verse. To an Englishman, Burns is an experience. There's no use pretending he isn't hard to understand when in his Scottish mode. I have heard his poems recited for an hour by a true devotee down in the Borders and didn't understand two percent.

Reading Burns yourself seems a little easier (better still with a glossary). He definitely repays the effort. There is a kind of revelatory triumph in arriving at comprehension with Burns because his sentiments turn out to be exactly what you feel—but didn't know how to put so well.

Burns liked mice. Today we would say he was green in his approach to these small creatures. In "To a Mouse," he apologizes to her for startling her—"On Turning Her Up in Her Nest With the Plough," November 1785. He sees no harm in the "wee, sleekit, cow'rin', tim'rous beastie" and wishes he could explain to it that it need see no harm in him. "Thou need na start awa sae hasty/Wi' bickering brattle!" he assures it. "I wad be laith to rin an' chase thee,/Wi' murdering pattle!" (A "pattle" is a plow staff).

The second verse needs no interpretation: "I'm truly sorry man's dominion/Has broken nature's social union, /An' justifies that ill opinion/ Which makes thee startle/At me, thy poor, earth-born companion/An' fellow mortal!"

Of course, Burns was a countryman. What he thought of city mice I do not know. The Scot in our urban dwelling, however, assures me he was a complete gentleman and loved all creatures of whatever class, and I have no reason to doubt it.

So what would he have done about our mouse?

We have had our mouse all through the winter. We have been careful to block up the gap under the door to the unlived-in part of the basement to make sure he knows his place. Sometimes, however, he's got through and reconnoitered the kitchen. Then one day, he—well, he came to a head.

I was in London. My wife was alone at home. She was watching TV in her study, which is on the lower level of our split-level house, across from the kitchen. On the phone, she sounded jittery.

"There's a rat!" she said, the telephone wires trembling slightly.

"A rat? Where?"

"It ran from under the house into the kitchen. It's enormous, and dark."

"How did it get under the door?"

"I don't know."

"How long is it? Six inches?"

"At least—seven or eight—it's enormous."

"Is that from tip of nose to end of tail, or is it his main body that is seven or eight inches long?"

"Oh! I don't know!"

I did my best to calm the situation. However, I began to realize my wife was going to demand action vis-à-vis rodents. And when I was home again, one evening the "rat" appeared outside her study door again. "There it is!"

Well—it was no rat. It was a mouse of customary "wee" build. It had a peek in the dog's bowl and then trotted over to investigate behind the kitchen sink. "You know mice really can't hurt you," I said. Later when I told friends about the two and a half inch "rat," the lady of the house said it must have seemed bigger because it went so fast: stretched out like a racing car. Terror can certainly play cruel tricks.

However, our mouse continued to stage guest appearances from the wings.

At this point, it should be explained that I have a strange distaste for killing animals. The conventional mousetrap was not to be considered. Various ruses were tried to woo our "beastie" into the outdoors. One was to leave the garage door ajar with a pile of peanuts strategically placed outside it. Then, after a suitable time, I would suddenly shut the door, and the mouse would be astounded to find himself locked out. The peanuts disappeared quickly enough, the door was closed, but the mouse was still inside a day or so later. Telltale rustling could be heard under a pile of wood in the garage, and the dog snuffed around excitedly but aimlessly.

Then one morning, I found our mouse deep in the back passage in the bin containing peanuts. He was happily munching. To get into the bin, he must have done a flying-trapeze act. To get out would have been impossible. In the meantime, he was not exactly facing starvation.

I arrested him politely, asked if he would mind spending a few moments in a slippery-sided plastic cereal box left nearby, and escorted him to the grassy area over the back-garden wall. In his nourished state, he raised no apparent objection. I launched him into his new career as a country mouse.

But we still had a mouse in or under the house.

"It looks," said I profoundly, "as if we have two mice. And one is still our lodger." I was not certain how to proceed.

Then one day, we wandered into a pet-and-garden shop in town. A large container displayed pet mice for sale. "This place likes mice," I thought.

I said to the assistant, "Do you know any harmless way of catching unwanted mice?"

She produced a small transparent plastic affair. "Like this?"

It's an ingenious invention. The mouse enters it with a view to the meal placed at the far end of a rectangular tunnel. As it approaches the meal, it steps on a small bar. This releases the little door at the entrance. With the door down, the mouse cannot escape but is perfectly safe and undamaged within.

I tried cheese first of all. The mouse went in, stepped over the bar without touching it, ate the cheese, turned round, stepped daintily over the bar again, and left. Next time, the door fell down—but before the mouse had entered. The third time, I put peanuts in. When I went to look later, the mouse was inside. And the door was shut.

"You and I," I said, as he beady-eyed me, "are going for a short journey."

In the long grass over the wall, he leapt for safety and vanished. I didn't even have time to quote Burns appropriately.

Mouse problem solved!

But just in case he was a wall-climber of the heroic sort with suction pads on his toes, I peanutted the "trip-trap" once more. In the morning, he was in it again.

However, after a closer inspection, I was sure it was not he himself, but a close relation. Something about this one's expression was different. His good wife perhaps? So I let her go where he had been freed and deposited a small pile of peanuts in the grass just to keep them going while they adjusted to their new life: a golden handshake.

And I put the baited trap ready again, its door poised in the open position.

The mouse it caught this time was smaller and browner. Definitely. I thought that since he was obviously not a close relation, he might like to seek new pastures farther afield. And so began a new routine....

With the dog's lead in one hand, and the mouse's mobile home in the other, I descend Sherbrooke Avenue and turn left down the lane to a nearby wild area, its summer grasses tall and dew-bespangled. Beneath an immature grove of silver birch, I open the door, and the morning's mouse creeps or scoots to freedom and an outdoor lifestyle.

To date, as I write, I have carried a total of 30 "fellow-mortal" mice to this distant habitat. Friends are skeptical. One believes it's all one mouse, following me back up the hill each day. She believes the local mice know me as "the peanut man." Another acquaintance thinks I'm merely making the mice vulnerable to "passing kestrels," thus substituting one fate for another.

But I think I'm just following in my Scottish grandmother's favorite poet's footsteps, and wishing no hurt to either one or three dozen small characters who have truly done me no hurt.

I'm sorry—of course—to be upsetting anyone's settled domestic arrangements ... but, as someone once said, "The best-laid schemes o' mice and men/Gang aft a-gley."

1992

Think Butterfly

It is hard to say when I last saw a butterfly. The fruit of city living perhaps?

I'm not sure though that it is just that. Butterflies may be almost as rare in the country now. Agricultural insecticides have radically contributed to the rarity of many kinds of wildlife. The destruction of hedgerows in Britain, to make larger fields, has widely obliterated habitats. Where have all the butterflies gone?

Some rural inhabitants take to the urban life. Foxes, for instance. Our local population increases in number and cheek every year—untroubled by sporadic bursts of ire from the canine classes. Some species of birds operate pretty successfully, too. But butterflies do not, as far as I can observe, take well to the notion of existence in the metropolis.

It's a truism though that you sometimes find what you are looking for and are more likely to see something you expect. Could it be that my eyes need butterfly training? It might be worth a try.

When I settled down in rural Yorkshire in the 1970s, I found that wherever I went, I continually encountered hedgehogs—but never at home.

I'd just come back from living in the eastern United States. A popular car sticker in American ski areas was "Think Snow." So I thought hedgehogs.

Soon they were virtually knocking at my front door. At night, strolling over the dew-wet, darkness-deep fields, I now had a new hazard to foot-placement. Once I almost tripped over a whole family of these delightful, prickly creatures. I spotted them with my flashlight just in time.

And just last week, here in Glasgow, I was bemoaning the absence from our garden of a favorite kind of bird, the wagtail. I'd spotted only one in 20 years. Two days later, I happened to be looking outside, and there on the damp paving stones was a wagtail doing what (true to their name) wagtails do.

But butterflies? Winter is hardly the time of year for them, though sometimes in a cobwebby corner of the house or shed, you used to come across a hibernating tortoisehell or peacock butterfly like a tattered toffee wrapper. Or even one fluttering dustily against the window glass, unseasonably energetic.

In the dim December days, thinking butterfly is a pleasantly contrary pastime. It is a foray into bright recollections.

It was my elder brother, smitten with birds, animals, and insects, who ensured that from the moment I was conscious, I was conscious of butterflies—of their names and markings and, above all, of their enticing color schemes. He chattered incessantly about them, and I saw no reason not to drink it all in. I also saw no reason to question his insect-collecting methods. These utterly fragile, powdery-winged creatures—the marbled whites, meadow browns, orange tips and clouded yellows—ended up as rows of meticulously mounted specimens in protective cases. It never entered my head that this arrangement might not be precisely what the butterflies had in mind. Or for that matter that such collecting might be discouraged in just a few decades.

I also had no reason to doubt that the exquisite delicate intricacies and panache of color and pattern, the bars and bands and speckles, and the veins and splotches were not meant entirely for my own visual pleasure. (Actually, I still half believe they are.) But it is by no means dead specimens that come back most vividly. On one occasion my brother somehow obtained a swallowtail chrysalis (or was it a caterpillar first?) and kept it carefully until the magnificent butterfly emerged.

Few metamorphoses are more exhilarating to witness. The discrepancy between packaged dullness and an airborne brilliance as weightless as a rainbow is breathtaking.

The British swallowtail is confined to a small habitat in the east country. Efforts are being made to conserve this butterfly. Some observers believe it is slightly on the increase.

Other butterfly memories return as inextricable associations with certain places. The violet panicles of the buddleia bushes in our garden in Bingley, for example, with their over-sweet honeyed scent, were the irresistible late-summer haunt of red admirals (so-called, though in fact they are red, black and white).The little holly blue belongs, for me, in the seaside resort of Scarborough. Here every summer we spent our childhood holidays. We rented a small beach hut—though actually it wasn't on the beach at all. To reach the beach, we climbed down steps and rocky paths of municipal contrivance.

It was among the parks department plants and rocks edging these steps that the holly blues fluttered and settled. If an entomologist were to challenge my identification of these butterflies, I might well collapse under hard questioning. I think my brother must have told me that's what they were. Now, looking in books, I have some uncertainty. Perhaps they were common blues?

Richard Adams, the author of *Watership Down*, told me in an interview that, walking in the country, it isn't the law that you must identify everything you see to appreciate it fully. I take heart from this. I remember a spectacular haven for butterflies in Norfolk. It was a low-lying field with large park trees—as if it belonged to some wealthy estate. Butterflies were everywhere, but I couldn't now name a single species we saw. Nor could I say just where the field is or when this took place.

All this memory jogging reminds me that I *did* see a butterfly not very long ago after all. Maybe two years back.

I suddenly caught sight of the splendid wings of a tortoiseshell sunning itself on a brick wall. It was magnificent. The late afternoon sun bathed wall and insect. With wings spread flat, it was utterly relaxed. Absorbed in the warmth, it might as well have been on the Riviera.

But it was not.

Its surroundings were tawdry and slummy. It was a neglected, grimy Victorian warehouse wall facing onto the railway lines. And the only reason I saw it at all, and then spent ten long minutes studying it, was that the train in which I was supposed to be traveling into Glasgow's Central Station was at an unexplained standstill. Public transport has its advantages after all. I was granted "time to stand and stare"—well, sit and stare at any rate.

And when we did eventually jerk into slow motion once again, I felt I'd had a rare experience. Here, perfectly unruffled by hammering trains, was a lone, gorgeously colorful member of the Nymphalidae family, living it up in urban wasteland.

An aristocrat at leisure.

2002

Hoots, Mon!

We can't be uniquely daft, can we? Surely we're not the only couple in the world who, watching a film on TV, have leapt up to answer the phone only to find it was ringing in the film?

We now try to avoid this occasional moment of domestic farce by first looking at each other questioningly, wondering. And then we rush for the phone because—this time—it's for real. But usually by the time we grab it, the caller has hung up.

It does seem that we probably are unique in another way. A few nights ago, we were lazily watching an old *Columbo* film (reruns seem prevalent again over here in Britain). During a nighttime episode, when the man himself in the shabby raincoat was investigating something in a suspect's house, an owl started hooting very loudly and repeatedly. We looked at each other questioningly.

"Is that in the movie?" I asked. "Why would they have an owl hooting? Doesn't seem like a *Columbo* background to me."

"I'm not sure."

She was sufficiently not sure to turn the volume down.

The owl continued to hoot.

It was so close to our windows that it might almost have been asking to come indoors. Perhaps it was perched on a window box. Its hooting seemed almost to be aimed at us.

This sort of behavior is not something that our neighborhood owls often indulge in. Well, never before, really. In fact, my distinct impression is that our owls—or is there only one?—are shy. I have only heard them hooting about once a year, on a night or two. I even wonder if they fly in to the area for a quick visit or actually live here.

Because evidence of them is so infrequent, their calls always send a minor thrill down my spine. I find owls strange. But I never think of them as spooky—though it does seem to be clear moonlight when they call out, which undoubtedly indicates a romantic attitude. To me, their call (and I am not talking about owls that shriek) is what Shakespeare called "a merry note."

My fascination for these birds started pretty early, at age five or six perhaps. My older brother introduced me to an owl pellet, found like a precious truffle in the leaves under an oak. Biology was not destined to be one of my favorite subjects at school. I was more in favor of school frogs being cut loose than being cut up. That was more my idea of experimenting with nature: let it be. But the owl pellet, containing all the precise, indigestible fragments of the owl's lunches and dinners, held me spellbound for some reason as my brother took it apart and laid it out on paper for analysis. Perhaps I hadn't yet learned to have fellow feeling for voles and small birds and beetles.

I first heard one of our local owls about six years ago. My ornithology wasn't up to knowing then that tawny owls, far from preferring remote rural habitats, actually like towns and enjoy the proximity of humans. Previous encounters with the species had been when I was living in farm country in Yorkshire. I'd notice them sometimes perched unsteadily on telephone wires in broad daylight, as if they had been caught out by the rising dawn and would now have to hold out uncomfortably until the relief of nightfall returned. They looked like fish out of water.

Another owl dive-bombed me from the big barn across the farmyard, presumably a defense display on account of a brood newly hatched or recently flown from the nest.

Then there was the flying white-faced owl that eyed me with a sidelong glare as I drove to evening class across the wild grassland. Those Yorkshire owls didn't much appreciate humans.

My immediate reaction on hearing my first Glasgow owl was simple incredulity. Here I was 10 minutes from the epicenter of Scotland's largest city, with the continuous roar of motorway traffic no more than half a mile away, and an owl was *hoo-hoo*ing, with happy abandon, close at hand but invisibly in the leaf-dark. I instantly put it down to pranking children.

But those "children" never seemed to grow up. More or less annually, for a night or two only, the *hoo-hoo*ing would suddenly recur. I began to think there really might be genuine owls around here after all.

And then, maybe three years ago, on Sutherland Avenue, I not only heard it once again, but I actually spotted it. I froze, holding my breath. It didn't move a feather. Our dogs waited with bored patience, wondering why I had been turned to stone. High up in a lime tree, perched, motionless, like a gowned lawyer, it stared down at me as coolly as I stared up at it admiringly. We were sizing each other up. I don't know quite what it made of me—

59

perhaps it had secretly seen me before, anyway—but it seemed to me to look remarkably knowing (or terribly wise as folklore often claims) and also a bit uncanny.

After some time it tired of this standoff, and deciding I was too big a mouse to digest easily, it flew to another tree with a gliding grace quite unexpectedly at odds with its tubby physique. And then it eyed me from there. After a while, it swung through the air to another tree farther off and started hooting again.

I felt peculiarly moved. Real life is so much more convincing than TV. Sorry, Columbo
2003

City Fox

Foxes have long been given what is known as "bad press." Book after book has presented them as sly and cunning. They may look like gentlemen, but hidden behind the smooth talk and the charm, lurks danger!

When Walt Disney wanted a plausible but wicked character to lead Pinocchio astray, he chose a fox. When Beatrix Potter wanted to trick a rather silly white duck in a poke bonnet, she chose a fox. When the Greek writer of fables, over 2,000 years ago, wanted an animal to represent cleverness or craftiness, he, too, chose the fox.

But Aesop also sometimes wrote about foxes as sad victims of circumstance; he saw that even this wily creature can be seen to have another side to its nature. We keep ducks in our back garden. So I must admit that we have developed a suspicion of foxes. This may strike you as odd when I tell you that we live in a city. But the fact is that foxes live here, too, and we have to watch out! City foxes, no less than their country cousins, have a taste for duck.... I happen to think that city foxes should know better.

Beatrix Potter and Aesop both wrote versions of "The City Mouse and the Country Mouse." These stories revolve around the idea that mice behave quite differently in these two quite dissimilar habitats. In the city, they depend on the waste provided (usually unwittingly) by the humans. In the country, they live by other rules and feed on food provided directly by nature.

The point is, of course, that everyone thinks of "wild" animals—even little ones—as naturally belonging in the country. If they set up in cities, it seems somehow unnatural. And yet vast numbers of people clearly think cities are the best place for people to live in—and more and more wild animals are following suit. At least, it seems like that; but maybe wild animals have always been city dwellers, or for centuries anyway, if Aesop's mousey "Citizen of the Town" is anything to go by. Either way, it isn't just that they stray into cities by mistake like Miss Potter's country mouse. They show every sign of actually preferring cities.

I've lived in the country and in the city. In the country, I saw wild animals and birds that I had never seen in a city: hares, badgers, curlews, owls. But the longer I live in the city, the more amazed I am at how much wildlife there is also living here successfully and with obvious satisfaction.

Admittedly, we live in a sort of suburb in the city. There are parks and golf courses all around, and the houses all have gardens, so there are plenty of trees and bushes. All the same, this is definitely city. A major highway runs along by a railway only a few hundred yards from our house, and traffic even on the larger side roads is frequent. Double- and single-decker buses pursue their routes nearby. Helicopters throb overhead, aircraft streak across the sky, and the whole teaming city of Glasgow, with its crowded roofs and endless crisscrossing lines of streetlights, is laid out across our view like a stage backdrop. Ibrox Football Stadium stands enormous down by the gas storage tanks, and on match nights, overwhelming crowds of supporters swarm in and take over the area (a different kind of wild animal!). As the match progresses, great surges of mass cheering or collective shock-horror (as goals are scored or yet another goal is missed) waft relentlessly through our windows. It's city all right.

Yet one morning at breakfast time, there was a heron balancing uncertainly on a small tree in a neighboring garden. One afternoon, there was a hedgehog running—a bit startled, it's true—along a sidewalk. Three weeks ago, three strange-looking birds, with crests on their heads, shared a spindly sapling on the bank by the highway, unaware, apparently, of the charging traffic; what kind of birds they were I have been quite unable to discover in bird books. I think some freak wind must have blown them off course.

Ten days ago, my dog and I both almost stumbled over a weasel scudding swiftly along the bottom of a garden wall and twisting sinuously through a gateway of the local private girls school to vanish in undergrowth. A student driver and her instructor saw it, too, and looked duly astounded, unable to believe their eyes. Fortunately, the car was stationary at that moment, so it didn't drive into a lamppost.

Recently, a particularly big garden just along our road has been colonized by a couple of gray squirrels. I often see them springing like trapeze artists from treetop to treetop, or leaping up trunks with arms and legs spread wide. I haven't seen a deer, but some neighbors have, on the road just outside their front door.

Only once have I encountered a rabbit around here. The reason may simply be the foxes. The foxes are our local raccoons (since raccoons don't live in Britain); they are the garbage bin rakers.

If there is one animal (apart from our mice, of course, and a multitude of common birds from pigeons, starlings, and sparrows to tiny red-breasted European robins, blue tits, chaffinches, wagtails, and wrens) that has really taken like a duck to water to city living, it's the fox.

Sleek and nonchalant, the foxes meander silently along the streets at night. They don't have a care in the world. If they wore hats, I swear they'd doff them to you (and your dog) and wish you a pleasant evening. Clearly, they are having a very pleasant evening as they take their nightly stroll.

They stop dead, sometimes, and observe us, standing in the widespread orange glow of the lights. Don't they realize we can also see them? Probably. They consider for a moment whether or not their chosen path might come just a little too close to ours for politeness's sake and then trot without any hurry into a garden or down a side turning.

We don't often see them in daylight, though I did a couple of months ago. Our ducks suddenly kicked up a silly racket. I looked out the bathroom window. They were circling on the pond, and the most gracefully slender red fox was poised on the bank ready to pounce. I banged on the window. It ignored the noise. I rushed down to the kitchen, opened the back door, shouted like a football fan, and slammed the door ferociously three times. He vanished. It was magic. I never saw him go. He was there. And then he wasn't.

Why, I wondered, should such a glorious creature be my enemy? Why can't he be satisfied with all the rich food waste he finds in everyone's garbage? He surely doesn't need, urban and urbane as he is, to kill to eat.

Yet I had to assume that he was the very same animal who, a week earlier, had done in one of the ducks and had eaten him for breakfast. I wasn't keen to share any more with him, though personally, I only eat the ducks' eggs.

Lately, some contractors have been laying new sewers along a bank between us and the railway. Three or four times a day, a siren sounds, and earthshaking reverberations, which make the house shiver, follow: underground blasting through sheer rock. Since I hadn't seen any foxes for some weeks, I had decided that this blasting had been too much for them and that they had moved house. Some city noises are apparently too much even for them.

But last night, while I walked the dog, my wife was sitting in the dining room looking out the window, and this fox came ambling through the garden. He left a narrow streak of prints like a ribbon to mark his passage—down to the lower pond, across to the hawthorn hedge, then back again to the corner of the wall over which he had made his entrance. When I came back from my uneventful walk, my wife told me what I'd missed. "He had no idea I was here watching him,"' she said. "Or else he just didn't care!"

I think he didn't care. When I lived in the country, I never once saw a fox. Yet everyone knew they lived up in the deserted quarry, and every so often they descended in the darkest times of night and wrought havoc among the poultry. The Country Fox is a hunted, cautious, invisible character. The City Fox … knows he's as safe as houses. I can think of no reason why he shouldn't declare an armistice with city ducks.

1991

New Pets

It's strange, but I've never been smitten with a great hankering to breed stick insects.

I don't know why this is so. It seems a perfectly natural thing to want to do. Indeed, my older brother was, at one stage of his boyhood and mine, smitten with such a hankering, and I (being four years younger) unquestioningly thought this was just one of the things older brothers do.

It strikes me now that maybe there were in fact a lot of older brothers whose interest in stick insects was, at most, minimal. But we had them in our family, and I grew quite fond of them, really.

Mind you, they don't run around a lot. Almost any other pet you can think of tops them in this regard. Even goldfish. We had two goldfish, called George and Margaret; we won them at the fairground by throwing wooden hoops over their bowls and carried them home jogglingly on the bus in jam jars, in trepidation about parental reaction. Though provided with a somewhat diminutive racetrack, goldfish lead a life of dash and thrill in their bowl by comparison with those stiff little stay-at-homes, stick insects. A tortoise (and ours was a master—or mistress, we were never sure—of the studied art of going nowhere with effortless immobility) was a streak of determined and frenetic activity compared to the stick insects. He would even occasionally (about once a year) venture his head out to take a cynical look at us, only to pull it in again in sheer fright. Stick insects, frankly, haven't latched onto fright as a notion.

In case you haven't come across a stick insect in your travels, a dictionary definition might not go amiss. "A stick insect is an insect with a long, thin body and legs. It looks like a small stick." I don't know if such insects grow much in the wild, but my brother's rigid wee pets, housed in an air-filled aquarium, weren't much longer than your average darning needle.

Perhaps they were nocturnal in their more active habits. But if so, they didn't keep us awake by bumping into things or rattling around like gerbils or hamsters. Even when we went to Scarborough for our summer holidays, bringing the stick insects along and having them in our bedroom, they let us sleep undisturbed.

It is possible, like the tortoise, that they didn't like to be watched. With him, they shared a propensity for eating in private. And with him also, they shared a conjuring ability to—vanish! In his case, though, he vanished more than he appeared, and after only living with us for a few months, he vanished one final time. Or she did.

My friend the artist Mary Newcomb remembers keeping stick insects as a child. "But," she assures me, hers were "cannibals." I don't recall my brother's brood diminishing conspicuously in this way, but maybe it did. Counting them was never easy—they looked so very like the stems of privet, which was their main food. I assumed they were vegetarian; but perhaps they sometimes mistook each other for a stem....

The one thing they did, and this was kind of interesting, was perpetuate their species. Their eggs were minuscule but quite distinct. And the hatched babies shared with all babies the ooh-ah aspect of being perfectly miniature versions of their adults.

That is about all I can think of to say on the subject of stick insects, and anyway it was only intended to lead up gently to the subject of worms.

I suppose some would argue that I am now one of those men who (theoretically) "has everything" and is therefore impossible to give birthday and Christmas presents to. And they might add that this salient fact explains why my wife gave me a clear plastic envelope full of tigerworms on my most recent birthday. I should say that this gift was the result of my enthusiasm, not hers, and it turns out that her willingness to pay for and order it denotes a not inconsiderable altruism. The very thought of them makes her squeam. I am roundly forbidden to keep them in the kitchen. So—in their firmly-lidded new home, which is like a large plastic garbage bin—they have taken up residence in the back passage of the basement that leads to the garage.

Some friends of mine have a New Zealand friend who also keenly keeps tigerworms in his house. When he recently came to visit in Scotland, knowing his appreciation of such matters, they took him on a tour of their garden to inspect their compost heaps. And therein lies a clue.

Tigerworms are the sort of worms that turn kitchen waste into what the pamphlet that accompanied my mail-ordered worms describes as "the caviar of composts." Once they are at home, they can consume all the waste from a family of four, not to mention shredded newspapers. Silently and (we are assured) without odor, they chomp away merrily night and day making wonderful rich soil to the immeasurable benefit of all kinds of horticultural endeavor. Or so we are promised.

"Can they escape?" asks my generous wife, possibly imagining that they are the stuff of horror movies and that the "tiger" in their name hints at rampant and rapacious inclinations.

It seems that she is not the first to ask this question. The Wormery Fact File (which I read out to her) is definite in its answer: "No, and if the Wormery is looked after as described, they have no reason to even try—it's a compost worm's paradise.... Once they have explored their new home, they tend to stay well out of sight in the compost ...."

I guess my new pets, then, are not exactly what you'd call Watcher Friendly. And even I don't think they are strokable. But they *are* a lot more useful than stick insects.

2002

IV.
Down on the Farm

A Serious Parade

The thing about geese is that they have dignity. Or at least they think they have—which is not necessarily, of course, quite the same thing. The thing about dignity is that it depends upon one taking oneself very seriously, and geese, or my geese at any rate, certainly do take themselves very seriously. This may explain why, the other morning, when I was standing in the farmyard laughing and laughing, the geese did not seem particularly amused.

Instead they eyed me beadily.

Still—I was, it is true, laughing directly at them, so perhaps it's understandable they didn't see the joke.

It isn't often one laughs out loud when no one else is around to join in (tears are more often a private matter), but on this occasion I simply couldn't stop myself. The reason was that the goose (as differentiated from the two ganders from whom she has been kept separate for the past five weeks) has at last hatched her brood—of one. She usually does better than that, but in spite of great concentration on the job, only one of her eggs has produced a youngster this year.

So the time has arrived for her to be let ceremoniously out of her confinement so that she may introduce her newcomer to the world, and, at the same time, to its two fathers. I give them both this title because both are absolutely sure, to put it in legal terms, of their paternity. Who knows?

They advance together across the yard and greet the mother and hatchling with long necks and great éclat. And then—the cause of my laughter—they, the Family Goose, proceed in parade-ground formation toward the gate, which opens onto the field that they consider their rightful domain.

Ken the farmer, who uses two of my buildings for his cows, describes this slow-moving formation as "the Protection Racket." The three adults surround the gosling. This small item of yellow-brown fluff on two legs, apparently unaware that it is no larger than any one of its parents' heads, scutters along with its own innate brand of mini-dignity, like some

71

surprisingly short president or leader threatened with assassination and therefore flanked on every available side by enormous, thug-like bodyguards.

Incidentally, I cannot imagine how the strange marching routine favored by the armies of dictators came to be called "the goose step." Nothing could be further from the *actual* way in which geese move. For one thing, their legs are far too short in relation to the rest of their bodies for them to try any such energetic sky-kicking. The truth is that they walk ponderously, their general weight lurching slow-rhythmically from one side to the other with every burdensome and flat-footed step. To each of these adult steps, the gosling does six or seven just to keep pace. And it squeaks anxiously all the time, while its elders attack the air with every lamellirostral imprecation imaginable: they hiss and honk and shout and squawk and yell and scream. The fact that no one has the least intention of attacking them or their baby is entirely beside the point. *Much noise* in the goose world is the best means of defense, and defense (in the goose world) is *de rigueur*.

The gosling is fortunate in being remarkably robust because the adults, in their almost competitive efforts to protect it, don't always watch where they are putting their feet. A sudden crescendo of squeaks usually means that one of these feet is standing on some or all of the gosling. But it doesn't take any hurt, waits for the great insensible foot to move off, rolls over a couple of times, and then races to catch up with its parents. They, in turn, are making such a fuss that they have no apparent idea that they have almost done in the object of their over-caring.

The hatching time of year is like weather—variable in mood. The farmyard seems literally to drip with fresh life. This season the bantams (never very strong on family planning) have once again escaped my periodic searches and produced large crowds of chicks in the most unexpected quarters. One batch hatched in an old plastic bucket ten feet above the entrance to the barn (I had to help them down using a ladder). Another lot appeared one morning out in the yard, fully hatched, in the middle of a rainstorm; I still don't know where that mother hen had been hiding.

But all this delighted production is rather grimly punctuated by disasters: abandonments, confusions, inadvertent losses, desperate squeakings, and dismaying silences. I always question myself: why is it that I feel this interplay of light and dark, of loss and gain, so piercingly? Why is it that the birds themselves—for the most part—do not? How is it that the fierce mothering instinct of the hen-birds is so concentrated on the more strong and able and is so comparatively indifferent to the fate of the less strong and able?

The senseless/sensible geese give no thought to such enigmas, and now, finally, their procession has reached the field. I swing the gate shut after them, and they can relax.

The gosling loses no time in learning that it is a goose and must do what geese do. They eat grass (not insects or snails). It can be watched out there in the meadow tugging away lustily at juicy blade after juicy blade, never far from its triumvirate of dignified but loud-mouthed guardians, and never for a *moment* questioning the perfectly natural fact that it—this year's star attraction—is the epicenter of the universe. And this, indeed, is a matter to be taken very *seriously*.

1980

My Dry-Stone Wall

Sometimes I look at my dry-stone wall, and a warmish feeling goes through me. It's not very long—the wall, that is—twenty to twenty-five feet, I'd say. And it does have a remarkable curve to it that a less indulgent observer than I am might notice places some stress on its equilibrium at one point, making its already sensitive relationship with the law of gravity somewhat more tenuous.

But I suppose, in all due modesty, that the feeling it gives me is a kind of pride. Not unimpressively, it has continued to stand, without apparent wavering, for several months now. After all, I *did* build it to last.

As it grew, stone by stone, friends had offered advice. Cyril (who helped me up with a particularly hefty rock) kept telling me not to forget the "through-stones"—stones that extend from side to side. In theory, and, for all I know in practice, too, these stones act to hold the different sides of the wall together. A dry-stone wall, which has no mortar in it, is in fact *two walls* running parallel to and leaning against each other for support. Between them is rubble infill. So I heaved up the occasional through-stone to tie these two walls to each other.

"And the wall should taper towards the top," Cyril further informed me. I did my best to approximate a taper.

Cyril's advice was the most practical I received—which is a little strange, since by his own admission, he has, himself, never actually *built* a single dry-stone wall.

Ken, on the other hand, has been building them since childhood. He took me to see a superbly keen and upstanding job he'd done years ago. "Be there after I'm gone," he said matter-of-factly.

The art of wall-building is so much in Ken's blood that to him it seems simply a matter of common sense. Questions of skill or technique probably don't enter his head.

Ken is the farmer who works the fields around my house. Our conversations—if this is the right word—take place for the most part with a field or two in between us. Since he has difficulty understanding my southern, and I have difficulty understanding his northern accent, these yelled communications tend to have the character of telephone conversations between mutual aliens on a particularly crackly interstellar line. Sometimes, the helplessness of our efforts gets too much for both of us, and we guffaw appreciatively at what we hope was the joke the other one was making and in the further hope that this will shorten the conversation before we both go hoarse. It usually does—though the thought of how many items of solemn import I have greeted with raucous out-of-doors laughter does sometimes concern me a little.

Anyway, Ken, observing from three fields away that my half-nephew John and I were starting to build a wall, bellowed: "Course 'em and curse 'em!"

"Do ... *what?*" we threw back. And to each other: "What did he say?"

"COURSE 'EM AND CURSE 'EM!" This time, an all-conquering bawl, it reached us.

"Oh—right—yes!"

This helpful dictum for wall-builders was followed by a thoughtful pause, while Ken grinned knowingly in our direction. Then—

"You know what to say?" he hollered. It was a purely rhetorical question, but he waited for a comeback from us.

"No—what?" we roared in concert.

"Squat!"

"*What?*"

"*SQUAT!*" (The word had a short "a" like "splat.") A cow mooed disapprovingly at all this inappropriate racket. "When you put t' stone down," Ken persisted, as if explaining the delightfully obvious to a pair of children, "you say 'SQUAT!'"

So—squat upon squat the wall grew. After the initial burst of effort with John, things went rather more slowly. He went off to Nigeria, which didn't help. (Ken's comment was: "*By!*—'e'll be'andling 'ot stones now!") But a few stones were added each day, and the wall almost seemed to build itself. Toward the end, Sue (visiting) placed a number of ladylike stones in different places, and suddenly it looked as though we were nearly home.

Now a herb garden, or its beginnings, is growing along one side of the wall—apple mint, borage, dill, chives, and lavender, as well as a clematis winding tendrilly in and out of its crevices. It needs aubretia to hummock over it, but this year has been too dry to establish any.

Actually, I have no possible justification for being proud. At hand and all around, lies humbling evidence of the littleness of this achievement. Rollicking dry-stone walls surround my croft—as they surround every field that's visible for miles and miles and miles. They span and stretch; they march and stride. They outline fields of all sizes and shapes. They net the landscape in an irregular but ubiquitous mesh, as if holding in place its heights and depths and contourings. They roll and undulate, following the mounds and hills. They climb sheer up (or down) the sides of near-cliffs, sometimes stopping dead on the very edge of a precipice as if the farmers who built them (When? In the 18th century? Earlier?) preferred their sheep to fall over than stray into a neighboring meadow. In fact, though, the sheep can climb most of the walls like mountain goats. You sometimes see them, like kings-of-the-castle, perched cockily on wall tops.

The walls are so much part of the landscape that it's impossible to visualize it without them. They seem as essential to the soft fields as bones are to a body. They seem to be the structure and skeleton of these endless meadows. But, in fact, they are imposed on them by the marvelous industry of humans.

These walls in the northern counties of England quite simply baffle the imagination. They can't be quantified. Think of the amount of sheer work, the endless exercise of hard muscle and rough-tough hands. Consider the thousands of millions of times a single wall-builder must have muttered "Squat!" under his breath—or, with feeling, somewhat more loudly, when a stone wouldn't do what it was bid or landed on his thumb.

This total partitioning of the land, this monumental defining of what was once wild ground, is so integral that it might as well be a natural phenomenon. These walls act—like the outcrops of rock, the soaring and echo-crying curlews, the suddenly sprinting hares, the twisting rush of the becks, and the isolated oaks and sycamores—as just one aspect of the way things are.

Something there is, as Robert Frost's mischief will have it, that doesn't love a wall. Not elves exactly—but I am certainly now wondering whether my inexpert stonework might fall victim to this winter's "frozen ground-swell." It does have its through-stones, though, and it does taper toward the top; but its cursed "courses"—to be quite honest—don't quite live up to the regularity suggested by that hopeful word. "A jumble of stones resting precariously on each others' backs" might come closer. At the very least, this piece of rural sculpture that I like to dignify with the name of "wall," has a certain amount of, well—of *settling* to do.

But we will hope. I have a feeling that the uncertainties suggested in Mr. Frost's much-quoted poem may not be the last word. I suspect that there is something that does, in fact, love a wall.

1972

Hercules Part 1

WE-ELL, I suppose it was inevitable.

The sheep, I mean.

After all, the house is getting so you can hardly move for baskets full of raw wool and skeins of newly spun and washed and drying wool and niddy-noddies and the spinning wheel and bags of lichen and tea-leaves for dying wool and an inkle loom for weaving wool and a sort of "know-your-sheep-breeds" chart to hang on the kitchen wall.

"His name," my wife announced in a tone that brooked no contradiction, "is *Hercules*."

It turned out that Hercules is not just any old sheep. He is on the "know-your-sheep" chart. He is unmistakably a *Herdwick*.

Now you may well be, as I was, a persistent believer that all sheep are pretty much just sheep—regular woolly creatures of tousled appearance, four legs, strange eyes, and remarkable silliness—and that they are creatures only too prompt to follow the crowd who panic mindlessly and always wait till the very last second before ambling across a moorland road in front of your car.

Let me assure you that once again, you and I are wrong. Sheep are not only classified into an astonishing variety of types, but they are also, one at a time, more than capable of idiosyncratic, individualistic behavior.

As to the types, one need only look at the wall chart. Their faces are as various as human visages. There's the Exmoor Horn, stocky and enigmatically smug, but not very bright; the Lincoln, spinster-auntish and smothered with braids; the North Country Cheviot like a particularly thuggish bull terrier; the Devon Longwool like a plump poodle. And the Herdwick. Of course, I could be biased, but I am beginning to think that the Herdwick is the only sensible-looking sheep there is, with its long gray-brown fleece, white face, and sturdy legs.

Herdwicks (according to a letter printed in a recent *Sunday Times)* have at least two unique traits. They are adept at forecasting snow because they have had a thousand years practicing this kind of thing high up on the Lake District

Fells and have apparently learned to provide themselves with an extra warm lining when needed in the severest weather—by swallowing some of their own wool. They are also reputed to have a vigorous homing instinct, always aiming to return to the place of their birth.

As for Hercules, he is certainly beginning to fit the bill for "individualistic behavior." Our relationship with him started when my wife found him sitting alone by a wall. He was the only Herdwick in a country-bred flock of no distinct variety. Either he wasn't going to be caught mixing with them, or they turned their backs on him. Either way, he seemed to be quite out of his element, and it had now evidently crossed his mind that merely kicking around a field eating grass by himself was scarcely worth the effort. So he simply stopped eating altogether.

For some time, my wife deliberately walked the dogs round that way and had a chat with this obstinate Herdwick on a hunger strike. She informed him that if he wanted a home, there was one ready and waiting just over there, by those buildings, three fields away.

But he still showed not the slightest inclination to eat or move.

Then one day, we were discussing him, and we decided we'd offer to look after him for the farmer. But before we did so—that very night—when my wife went to shut the door of the henhouse, she thought she heard a creature breathing deeply in the dark interior. She came back to the house for a flashlight and said, "There's an animal in the henhouse, and it isn't a hen."

It was—Hercules. He'd finally accepted her invitation.

Since then, he has been one of the more demanding preoccupations round here. We've lifted him onto his feet and commanded him to eat. We've given him hay and water and cow cake and sheep cake (only drawing the line at chocolate cake). We've stripped the crop of curly kale for him, alternating it with spinach leaves, which he gobbles with a fascinating mobility of the jaw. He has, over the winter, become completely tame.

For some weeks, we were giving him continual encouragement, putting him in the henhouse at night or letting him stay outdoors, but under an old door propped against a wall, or even lifting him into the back porch. All this solicitousness was met at first with perfect indifference. But slowly, he started to hint by canny and sheepish signs that he quite enjoyed the attention.

And now! Well—he's all over the place, moving with determined speed, eating, and eating. We never quite know where he's going to be next. When my wife goes out hunting for him, he rushes to her, eager to see what she has to offer.

Is he thinking of heading back to the Lake District in search of his ancestral roots? Or does he feel his new home, its boundaries expanding each day, is not so bad after all?

One thing is evident: he is beginning to live up to his name. He no longer droops like Holman Hunt's *Scapegoat* and no longer eyes us out of his pasty-clown face with the stolid, resigned self-pity of an Eeyore. He looks equal to any number or Herculean Labors. The Nemean lion wouldn't stand a chance.

His fleece is flourishing. The weavers and dyers in the house are eyeing it hopefully. I wonder how he'll take to being shorn? Will he object? Will he feel sorry for himself? I doubt it. But perhaps it is a good thing my wife didn't name him *Samson*.

1978

Hercules Part 2

We thought we'd pay Hercules a visit—Hercules, the great brown sheep who had gone on hunger strike.

We'd tended him all through the winter months, got him onto his feet again, fed, and even housed him for a while in the back porch.

He had become surprisingly tame. At our insistence, he eventually started to eat cattle food and curly kale. He would shove his surprisingly gentle muzzle into our cupped hands, munching away like a habitual gum-chewer with increasing relish as the year gradually woke out of its winter doldrums.

He came to life again in the same natural way that spring comes to life.

And then one day, he leaped up onto a field wall, leaped down the other side, and headed rapidly for the main road to The Lake District, the habitat where he, a Herdwick, anciently belongs. We found him eventually, wandering about on the road, and brought him back. But he was like a new sheep—a new sheep with travel plans.

There followed a period where this creature that we had tried so hard day after day to get moving, presented us instead with the daily problem of *curtailing* his movements. He was particularly taken with the idea of wall leaping. *We* were particularly taken with the idea of discouraging this.

At long last, he took the hint. He decided that it might, after all, be all right to settle down with us where we lived (rather than in the Lakes). He was joined by four Herdwick half-breeds newly purchased by Ken, the farmer who worked the fields around us. He became quite self-controlled. He and they grazed the surrounding fields happily together. They were even tolerated by the other non-Herdwick sheep who vastly outnumbered them.

One day, Ken informed my wife that he had decided to take all his sheep over to his father's farm a couple of miles away for some fresh grazing, and Hercules, quite happily, was to go along, too.

So we didn't see him for a couple of months, and then came that evening when we thought—as I said—we'd like to pay him the visit.

81

It was the kind of evening that I most love in this Yorkshire hill country: when the clouds build heavy-black with rain, but the breaks in them are a counterpoint of bursting gold; when everything is trembling with change, and stretches of light and shadow race each other over the fields; and when the soaked grass is an ocean of windy agitation. I confess that I see all this in terms of sheer *glory*.

Ken's father and mother live in a farmhouse that seems to have taken on their own atmosphere of coziness and domestic security. The immediate meadows appear always greener than those near our own house. I suppose they really aren't, but they might well have been trimmed and trimmed for centuries by the continual solicitude of generation upon generation of sheep, and that has an effect on the quality of grass.

There, down by the kitchen garden, was the mighty Hercules with two of the other Herdwicks. We knew him straight off, the friendly old gum-chewer. We yelled to him.

He continued to chew determinedly.

I believed he hadn't stopped chewing for the whole intervening time since we last saw him. His girth had doubled, and his still unshorn fleece had filled out remarkably.

"Hercules! Hercules!" we yelled in unison. "HER-CU-LES!" We didn't feel too ridiculous—Ken's parents, who would certainly have thought calling a sheep by name very peculiar—were out. Hercules finally looked up. We expected him to come running at the sound of his name, as he used to, galumphing weightily across the ground to see what tidbits were on offer. Tonight (and it was starting to rain now) he just—munched. And then, he simply ambled off with complete disregard, still munching.

He never did come. I think we both felt a certain mingling of admiration and sadness; finally he had struck out on his own, his dependence on us gone. After all, why on earth should one look for gratitude from an animal?

We drove back home. An episode had finally closed. We had done what we could, and the reward for the effort was in his robust—indifference.

Next morning, my wife told Ken we had been over to his father's place to see Hercules.

"He took no notice of us at all," she said.

"No wonder," Ken replied, grinning, "he isn't down at me father's. He's up t' other side of *our* 'ouse. Nay, lass, and you call yourself a *shepherd*!" And although I wasn't present, I feel sure he shook his head knowingly.

He brought all the sheep that were behind his house down here to the fields

A Word or Two

round our house a few days later. And among them was the *genuine* Hercules. He was just as gargantuan of stature and full of self-confidence as his mistaken counterpart.

But there was one difference. This time, when he heard his name, he *came running.*

1978

The Great Midnight Milk Run

There is a rural myth—at least I believe it's a myth—that hedgehogs, in the long hours of darkness, sometimes treat themselves to a drink of milk from cows as they lie asleep in the dewy meadow grass.

Originally, perhaps, it was an old wives' tale to explain why certain cows were not yielding as much milk as expected come the morning.

It's as good an explanation as any, really. And if it wasn't for the notable absence of hedgehogs in our neck of the city of Glasgow (in nine years here I've only seen one, and that was belting along a sidewalk at high speed one afternoon as if it had strayed into the city by mistake and wanted to return to country living as soon as possible), I might be tempted to apply the same explanation to the mysterious and frequent disappearance of our milk supply.

The only difficulty, however, is that our particular hedgehog milk-stealer would have to be living secretively behind the refrigerator and be equipped with a laser-like straw that could penetrate sheet-metal, incrustations of permafrost, yogurt cartons, and plastic-covered wedges of Orkney cheese—not to mention the milk jug itself—in its direct and deadly pursuit of our milk. But how else *can* one account for the regular absence of pints of milk that we thought we had in there?

Darkness has something to do with it. It's always midnight—and after *she's* already gone to bed—that I discover we are once again out of milk. Breakfast without it is, of course, an unthinkable catastrophe; so, sighing with dramatic emphasis, I head off in the car to the filling station on Paisley Road West, just across the way from the betting shop and the bar by the traffic lights on the road that leads down to Ibrox Football Stadium.

Open 24 hours, this useful garage-cum-emporium is, and it supplies milk as well as gasoline, not to mention compact discs and one-size tights and sliced bread and cans of oil and fanbelts.

Actually (though don't tell anyone, as I like to give the impression that running out of milk at midnight is a *terrific burden* that only the most long-suffering husband would willingly bear), these little nighttime trips give me a funny, if peripheral, sense of enjoyment. Possibly it's the schoolboy in me—an echo of the memory of secret late-night feasts in the dormitory at school, second only in clandestine excitement to pillow fights.

Sometimes I sit in the car at the filling station and munch my way through a packet of smokey bacon potato crisps before I chug back over the motorway bridge, past the bowling club and the artificial ski slope in the park the Pope visited a year or so ago (the park, that is, not the ski slope), over the railway, past the hotel, and home again—with the milk.

But also part of the fun is, I think, the *contrast*. The trip takes me "across the tracks"—and the difference between one side of the tracks and the other is palpable.

Our side is quiet, and although only a ten-minute drive from the city center, it is a kind of suburb within the city. Other than the occasional swish of a Porsche or Mercedes along one of the lime-lined avenues—a teenager late home in Dad's borrowed car—this area is, by that time of night, dead to the world. The lurid orange streetlights illumine an emptiness. Maybe one late dog walker, maybe one of the resident bin-raiding foxes, is ambling by— but usually not a soul.

The filling station, no more than a mile, if that, away—is city proper. It's something of a local meeting place, just livening up at midnight, for kids who can't see any sense in sleep. It's brightly lit. Motorbikes rev. Everyone's laughing, joking, yelling, and flirting in the queue at the shop window (the door is locked by then for security) to buy a bottle of "Irn Bru" or "ginger" or tomorrow morning's tabloid rag—or a carton of milk and a packet of smokey bacon crisps. I don't *need* the crisps in the least, of course, but something— probably just amusement, possibly something profoundly urban in my makeup—makes me want to stay around there for a minute or two before I go back to the urban-suburbia where I … belong? Well, where I live, at any rate, and on the whole, I have to admit, very satisfactorily, really.

There may, however, be something else at the back of my pleasure in these milk trips. I've only just realized what it might be. It may be a way of continuing something from the past in different form; something, in fact, *rural* in city form.

For a decade in the 1970s I lived quite deeply in the country, down in Yorkshire. And there, collecting the milk was an event. Intriguingly, this also often took place at bedtime, when I'd discovered there wouldn't be enough for breakfast. I also had to fetch it then rather than in the morning, unless I was prepared to go to the farm at some unearthly and very early hour to get there before the milk tanker came to transport its load of creamy liquid to the dairy in the market town five miles away.

This farm milk hadn't arrived anywhere near the bottle or carton stage yet. It was still in the container, and I had to dip my galvanized metal can into this container. It had left the cow very recently indeed. If I went for it too soon after milking, it would still be warm.

My city visitors would be sent to fetch the milk as a rustic adventure—most of them returned safely—but generally it was my job, and generally the flashlight wasn't working yet again. This lack of light mattered because—and this is something soon forgotten in the city—it is astonishingly dark in the country.

Today, in Glasgow, I'm conscious that I never experience out-and-out darkness. I'm sure I should be grateful; streetlights are one of the basic evidences of civilization. But it seems more than a shame to me that city people don't experience the exhilaration, the odd mix of secrecy and danger, that the total darkness of the countryside provides.

Of course, moon and stars often interfere with this velvet blackness, but when they do, the rural view of them is still entirely different from the urban view because—apart from the sporadic spark of a farmhouse window still lit here and there—the earth becomes a black and empty space, and all the activity is up there above your head. The vast, encompassing arch of the sky predominates because there is no competing light, and the ground is simply the pitted and wrinkled receptacle of that intangible, weak, silvery glimmer.

One night, in a light misty rain, I saw a moonbow—if that is its proper name—a rainbow by moonlight. I leaped about like an excited calf (there was nobody there to watch me; the *real* calves were in the barn). I imagined colors in it, but I think they weren't there at all. To be more objective, I'd say it was probably composed entirely of magical gradations from pitch black to cool white brightness. I don't really expect to see such a subtle phenomenon in the well-lit city.

Fetching the midnight milk was often a grumbling matter, particularly in drenching rain, but its very difficulties and hazards belonged to the country so totally that as an activity it seems to epitomize the difference between the city and the country.

After successfully crossing the paddock-cum-garden to the corner of the wall, I had to poise the empty can precariously on the uneven top of the wall, which then had to be climbed. This minor form of mountaineering is a technical feat, involving deft balance and footwork. It is best done in daylight. Because it is a dry-stone wall, without mortar of any kind, not all footholds are reliable, and even stones at the top that have been stable for a couple of centuries have a sudden capacity for dislodgment. I have landed literally face-down in mud over these walls more than once—glad that such ignominy was not witnessed except by cows and sheep.

Next you need to know, and if possible avoid, the places where the mud is squelchiest as you tramp over the field up to the farm. You soon learn that wherever a tractor has been is likely to be a deep-rutted quagmire akin to the trenches of World War I, and that cows and tractors both render the ground at gateways impassable except in an amphibious tank. The cows also haphazardly spend their days making the fields into minefields. The wariest walker will inevitably tread in generous cakes of cow-donated ground enrichment.

The nighttime milk-collector-*without*-flashlight can, of course, avoid nothing. He just bravely walks on regardless.

At the farm, there is the garden to negotiate—a tangled wilderness of tall wet grass, currant bushes, lilac and mock-orange, flower beds, a discarded scythe, a broken-down lawn mower, a child's bike underfoot, and washing lines at neck level ready to garotte you. In icy weather, the sheets hanging from these can be like stiff cardboard. You duck and weave through all this. Then—not wanting to wake Ken and Biddy and the family—you tiptoe past the back door hoping the sheep dog doesn't hear you and bark like a coyote.

But, of course, she does, and she does. "Shhhh! Gwen!" you hiss desperately. "It's only me! Shut *up!*" But it's too late, and you know they know, and you know they'll twit you about it tomorrow.

Then into the cooling parlor, and *clang, bang,* you fall over a conglomeration of metal shovels and rubber tubes and pipes, and at last you plunge your container lightly into the thick, yellowy depths and lift it out heavily, coated and creamy and dripping. You've got what you came for—90 percent quadruple-grade cream plus a little bit of milk.

The journey home is no less hazardous, except you have the blurry distant light from your own house as a vague kind of target. Above you is all the openness of the universe. It is, even in what you can see with your naked eyes, so inconceivably large as to seem—*daft.* I mean, *why*, in heaven's name, is it all up there? What's it all for?

Some sheep stare at you in an indignant huddle, furious in a woolly-minded, not very committed fashion, at your intrusion. They don't stop grinding their mouths from side to side, but they eye you.

Then your own dog—who has theoretically come with you, but in fact gone rabbit chasing in a hedgerow three fields away—returns without announcement and scrabbles over the wall in a moment, narrowly missing the scrupulously balanced can of milk you have just placed there. It wobbles, about to fall, but you grab it in the nick of time. You balance it again, heave yourself over, and head at last for the back door. It is all part of the routine— you are, as usual, shaken, mud-bespattered, your boots are caked, and they are smelly with dung. But your head is singing with the overwhelming stimulus of air and country living and darkness and being *gloriously alone*.

The moral? Well, there isn't one really—except maybe a question and an answer.

The question is: Who has it best when obtaining milk at midnight, the city-dweller or the country-dweller?

And the answer is: hedgehogs.

1990

Departing Delight

Delight is not usually found in goodbyes. But the departure of our wild ducks could only be called delightful.

I'm not sure now, but I think it was the farmer next door who discovered the clutch of five eggs in among the bluebells on the bank of the beck that ran below his farmhouse. He suggested I put them under a broody hen. The act of boyish thievery strikes me, now, as shameful; but I put them under a silly hen who warmed them to hatching and in due time solicitously mothered them around the yard.

We once had a goose, reared by us, who thought herself human. These newcomers, the wild ducklings, thought themselves chickens, destined to grow into adults resembling their "mother." Until, that was, they made a surprising discovery when they suddenly marched into the pond in the corner of the yard. First, they went to the edge for a drink, then farther in for a paddle, and after that (it just seemed natural somehow) launched into the deep to float, dip, and dash about on the water's surface, erratically straining their fluffy yellow necks up for insects.

This was the beginning of their mother washing her hands of them. Her indignation was scarcely containable. She clucked and scratched in the grit and earth on shore. What in heaven's name is the younger generation coming to? Don't they know they are chickens? But one thing was certain: *she* was not going to get her feet wet! Only foolish mothers copy their young.

Through the early summer, the ducklings grew, and their mother became more and more disappointed in them. Having discovered the pleasures of aquatic diversion, they were not to be kept away from the water—and, even worse, they started to associate with the domestic ducks and ducklings that splashed endlessly in the same washy place.

So the time came when the hen went back to her kind, and the five wild ducks belonged to themselves.

Then, one day, I noticed there were not five but *six* wild ducks on the water.... The implications of this arrival were profound.

At last, toward dusk one evening, it happened. The six wild ducks rose together and flew up the field, quite low, in a full circle, to land back on the water again in a chaotic display of inexperience. It was obvious that this new dimension—flight—had taken all five by surprise. Not the sixth, however. She knew what this was all about, oh yes: *wild* ducks fly.

The initial training flight was repeated the next evening in a slightly wider circle and a little higher. And it recurred in increasingly wider circles each evening after that. It became perfectly clear what was going on. We did not know when the moment itself would come, but we were sort of ready for it. We didn't want to miss it.

I had taken to leaping melodramatically onto the slate slab by the wall just outside the kitchen door for a better view of the evening flights and … *this* time I watched in delighted awe as the six wild ducks flew seriously high, wings beating strongly, at ease in their native air, making a loose formation against the light of the sky.

Their circle was wider in its curve than ever before. And then the curve began to straighten a little. They headed up over there toward the quarry—over the quarry—and, for the first time, *out of sight.* We took a deep breath. And we knew that this circle was the one that would never come back on itself.

1994

V.
Encounters

An American in Edinburgh

He was, I guessed, what the novelist Graham Greene called a "quiet American." Certainly he sported an extremely pressed and clean striped shirt with a button-down collar. His green-beige socks did not slouch. His hair was organized. There was nothing scuffed about him. He had probably showered recently in one of Edinburgh's less-inexpensive hotels.

By his evidently fastidious standards, however, I suspect that this young man was casually dressed—as befits attendance at an arts festival.

To get a seat near the platform, I had arrived as early as possible. He—sitting on the left-most seat in the front row—had taken up residence even sooner.

We sat at right angles to one another. I was in the front row of the side seats. If he had shown any signs of conversation, I would not have been opposed. But he showed no signs. In fact, his eyes looked away. But then he seemed to be looking at me—almost staring inquiringly—only to turn away the moment I looked at him. This happened more than once, and I tried not to show any puzzlement. There seemed to be something not quite at ease about him.

The audience filled up the rows behind him.

In 25 minutes, the German theatrical director Peter Stein was to be interviewed on the platform by one of Britain's leading drama critics. Fifteen minutes went by, and now the seats were packed, and more people started to sit on the stairs at the back and even on the balcony above.

Mr. Stein's reputation at the Edinburgh Festival had already been built by productions in two earlier years, and this year his slow, sultry, and atmospheric *Uncle Vanya* had opened the night before.

Now there were only five minutes to go. Stein must be about to appear. All the seats were taken. Expectation was in the air—but then something entirely unexpected happened.

The quiet American stood up. I was a little surprised. But when he proceeded to turn around and face the chattering audience, my surprise grew

93

bigger. And when he lifted up a placard in both hands, faced it toward the audience, and slowly moved it in an arc so that it would be clearly seen by every single person therein, surprise gave way to downright astonishment.

The passage of his placard, like the moon across the night sky, had a wondrous effect on those who could see it from the front. Their expressions changed. A flickering of smiles spread like a moving patch of light as the placard came into view. They mouthed the word written in large capitals on it. Then I caught a glimpse of it: the word was "MIMI."

The young man was now moving his message slowly forward and back, then holding it higher so it could be seen by the farthest row. Finally, just in case someone in the place had failed to notice it, he displayed it once more to everybody. Then he sat down again.

Now I looked at him straight, questioningly.

"It took me 20 minutes to get up enough courage to do that," he said with a grin.

"Who's Mimi?"

"She is this girl who lives in London. She's a friend of a friend of mine. I've never met her—so I have no idea what she looks like. I do know she is planning to be at several festival events and productions I am going to, and I am absolutely determined to meet her." He paused. "I have been phoning her from New York"—*Ah*, I thought silently, *you're a New Yorker; that explains a lot*—"for the past week, but her line is always busy. I never reached her."

"Well, I wonder if she is here," I said, "but doesn't want to admit it."

"Yeah, maybe she's too shy to stand up. Well, there are two or three other events when I can try again…. Do you think there'll be time for questions?" he changed the subject suddenly. "I have some I really want to ask."

Peter Stein is a talker. His interviewer hardly got a word in. It was fascinating, and the hour was soon nearly up. Michael Billington (the interviewer) at last managed to intercept the flow and suggest questions from the floor.

"Why do you concentrate so much on the established classics—Greek tragedies and Chekhov?" a young woman at the back asked. "Aren't there any contemporary playwrights that you want to direct?"

"Well, most of them aren't as good as Aeschylus," Stein replied. "And at my age, how many more productions can I still expect to do? There are so many great plays I would still like to direct…. "

The questioner was insistent. "Are there no living writers you admire—surely?"

"Well, yes: Botho Strauss." Apparently his fellow countryman was the only one.

There were other urgent questions, one after another, but the quiet American—eagerly waving his hand to catch Mr. Billington's peripheral vision, starting even to call out excitedly—was still waving when the interview was brought to an end ten minutes later than scheduled.

Stein and Billington got up and walked through the applauding audience, heading for the lift.

"I have to get his autograph before he reaches the elevator. Excuse me!" said the quiet American with desperate urgency. He leaped up, tripped over his seat, barged into several backs, and launched himself Steinward while trying to regain his balance. I sensed that this was one ambition-of-the-moment that he was definitely *not* going to forego.

"Sir! Please, sir! Would you …?" I heard him cry loudly through the rising babble of the departing audience.

And then I heard Stein's German accent, affable and delighted: "Of course! It would be a very great privilege.… " *Thank goodness,* I thought.

I watched for the slowly circling "MIMI" placard at other festival events but never saw it again. Nor did I see the perhaps-not-quite-so-quiet American, accompanied or unaccompanied. I hope they did meet.

And I hope that Mimi—well, I hope that she has a good sense of humor and is not easily embarrassed.

1996

Someone's Got to Cha-Cha

I have grown to be not immodest about my prowess as a ballroom dancer. Those who have felt the brunt of my efforts, as it were, in the region of their toes and shins, might well say "with good reason."

But the truth is that there was a callow time when I felt pretty certain I did a rather nifty quickstep. I was particularly keen on the negotiation of corners—an inventive concatenation of progressive and regressive moves at lightning speed that was designed to make the rest of the room look like snails—followed by an alarmingly independent line of footwork surging from one end of the place to the other with my partner unexpectedly swept backward off her feet en route.

Not that I have lost the knack or anything. It's just that on the decreasing number of occasions in recent times when I have been called upon to take the floor, I seem to have become less impressed by my performance than I used to be. The fact is that even in my busier dancing years, I was really more an admirer of others—and consequently only a somewhat pale imitator—than I was a true originator.

And I fear that my wife is nowadays keener on disco dancing than on waltzes and foxtrots. In our few attempts together at such passé social practices, our ankles have tended toward mutual confusion, so perhaps it is better, in the end, to dance with each other in different parts of the room.

Not that one's disco style has much more to recommend it than one's tango. I never mastered the tango, in spite of its being on the agenda at the dancing lessons (for 15-year-olds) I attended in Camberley.

I have retained only the slightest after-image of its magnificent elongations and sudden twists of fortune. Was it the tango that our teacher said should be danced entirely as if one had a newspaper between one's knees? Maybe that was the rumba. I even fancy that she supplied us all with copies of the *Camberley News* to prove her point, and that newsprint came off on our various legs, and paper shredded disconsolately all over the bare boards of the scout hut.

But the tango (or rumba) still slipped my grasp. When it came to less formal types of dancing—the type accompanied by such devastatingly volumetric music that even yelled conversation is no longer possible—it wasn't then called "disco"; it was called "jive."

It was at Guildford Technical College that I learned to jive, if you can call my version of it by the orthodox name. The college was annexed to the Art School, and it was from this neighboring den of aesthetics that the more fabulous jivers emerged. Clearly they had been practicing for decades. This sort of thing has always been an enigma to me: how can people who apparently have only 18 years or less under their belts nevertheless achieve skills that call for a lifetime to acquire?

And where, I asked myself, had I been all my days that I had learned only a hesitant waltz with reverse turns and couldn't pick up a partner (wearing a full skirt and a Marks-and-Spencer cardigan buttoned down the back, her hair flying out in a ponytail) and throw her with negligent ease over each shoulder in ice-swift succession, twirl her like a spinning top by an ingeniously serpentine series of under-and-over-and-under-arching arm movements, and push her vigorously away only to have her spring back at me as if we were both made of elastic?

I observed the jive wizards (who accomplished this and more) with wonder and waited for a crowded and darkened room to make my own attempts with whatever long-suffering girls were willing to waste their own superior expertise on my practice sessions. The best I managed was a kind of simplified formula. I was never satisfied with it.

Today, I suppose, disco dancing is a kind of pale residue of real jive. It is a lot easier for everyone but seems to me to lack drama and panache somehow.

And has the art of ballroom dancing today also died a death? I know from television that competitive ballroom dancers are still alive and well and covered in sequins somewhere in Hammersmith or Bournemouth. These dedicated amateur-professionals pursue their chocolate-box calling with such undivided enthusiasm that, in some cases, it is fast approaching a High Art. It is becoming Torvill and Dean without the skates, Rogers and Astaire without the clapperboards.

But what about the real world? Well, I'm glad to report that we have four close friends (two married couples) who are keeping things going masterfully.

Mysteriously, it may have something to do with the transatlantic alliance because the wives in both cases are from California. The husbands are Scottish and English, respectively.

The scene where they trip the light fantastic and shimmy the nights away is Scotland. They are most obliging. With little prompting, they will form up—in the sitting room, on Princes Street, anywhere—and demonstrate their latest steps. They can do the tango (though they don't seem to have heard of the newspaper trick).

One couple is attending classes twice a week at present, the Beginners and the Advanced. The other I suspect—though I haven't asked them—are simply Advanced. They certainly were about a year ago when they and my wife and I all had a Saturday evening meal together in a small Scottish country town.

The pub turned out to have a dance floor, about the size of two Ping-Pong tables side by side. It was already filled with couples, and they were clearly regulars. I guessed they came here with their wives once a week and were probably farmers and insurance salesmen and representatives of sheep-dip suppliers. What they didn't know was that Fred and Ginger—being urged on by mischievous friends wanting to witness a spectacle—were quietly eating pork chops at one of the side tables.

"Go on," we whispered, "this is your big opportunity."

Our friends didn't take much persuading. They stood up and slid with consummate grace to the starting position. They set themselves incisively. She gazed up at him; he gazed straight ahead. They started to count, visibly but silently. And then—they launched.

Well! Lessons do make a difference! Here was no amble, no aimless mingling in the melee.

These two sailed with immaculate ease and exact timing, describing a splendid pattern on that small dance floor that seemed to have been predetermined by the inevitability of the preceding centuries. This, their cha-cha, was like no cha-cha-cha ever done before-before. It swept all before them.

Eventually, as the music lulled, the bemused locals simply stood and applauded. It wasn't in the least ironic. It was just superiority given due recognition. Our friends returned to Black Forest gateaux, flushed with success and laughter. We naturally voiced our admiration.

Just the other day, the other couple asked us if we would like to come to lessons with them. Actually, they asked my wife. It seems the lessons needed some extra support. But she declined. Our already full schedule made it impossible.

"Anyway," she said as she told me about it afterward, "it isn't really our scene, is it?"

"No, no, of course not," I said.

But I thought secretly that she may also have been a touch concerned for her toes and shins.

1986

Live Ringers

I can't say I have been much inclined, until now, to place bell ringing among the more adventurous, or even dangerous, of occupations.

But then it's true that I hadn't given it much thought. A recent evening with members of the Towcester band of church bell ringers or "change ringers"—my journalistic aim was to try to grasp something of the technicalities of this redoubtable English ethnic art—has, however, caused a certain revision of opinion on this score.

Always eager for a good story, I press the ringers for any they might have. We are assembled, after an impressive rehearsal in the 15th-century church tower down the road, in the Saracen's Head (which used to be much visited by Charles Dickens and which he used as the setting for an incident in *Pickwick Papers*). The chief claim to fame today of this inn on Watling Street (one of the roads the ancient Romans unwittingly bequeathed to the motorists of the 20th century) may be its eye-catching notices on the pavement. They are designed to announce lunch or dinner. When the latter is ready for customers, for instance, the word "dinner" is appropriately inserted in the middle of this notice. Likewise lunch. But in the time between these gustatory events, when the kitchen staff is off duty, the space is simply left blank. The result (which has not been ignored by national television) is a sign that reads: "Saracen's Head Now Being Served."

The bell ringers are a sociable lot. But while they are actually ringing, the intense concentration required by the process makes for a high seriousness. With some ringers, as their arms go rhythmically up and down, up and down, an expression suggesting bemused contemplation can settle over the features. "Just imagine," one of them says, "ringing for three hours! You can't even blow your nose."

And three hours of ringing is, indeed, an achievement *expected* of ringers of five or more bells—ringers who are worth their salt. Such a stint constitutes a "full peal" and involves more than 5,000 "changes" in the order of the notes. Even a quarter peal is a worthy aim, and is, rather naturally, more often attempted.

"Attempted" is right because sometimes "awkward happenings" can occur. On one recent occasion, for instance, a young lad, just starting to learn "change ringing," managed to let his bell swing too far. It went over the top, broke the ash wood stay (which is *meant* to break so that worse damage isn't done to the bell itself, not to mention the bell tower and bell ringers below)— and up went his rope. An experienced ringer would, at this point, have let go. He, however, did not. He hung on and went up with the rope 15 feet, and only when he realized his knuckles were about to make contact with the ceiling beams, did he consider it perhaps preferable to release his hold.

Jon Lovell, the ringer who tells me this story (and a hero by any standard), had been ringing next to the lad. By now, however, he had adroitly positioned himself under the descendant boy in order, charitably, to break his fall. The boy was, in fact, unhurt—though there was something about the occurrence that seems to have persuaded him to try other kinds of sport.

This isn't, however, the best story of the evening. The story of Bill's trousers beats it into a cocked hat.

Bryan takes up the tale.

"We were ringing a quarter ... "

"It was a *full peal*," Janet corrects him. [Laughter.]

"Sorry—a peal," Bryan goes on, "and there were six of us ... "

"*Eight* of us,'' corrects Janet. [More laughter.]

"And we'd been ringing for about 20 minutes ... was it?"

"No! We'd been going for about an *hour*!" [Most laughter.]

"Were you *there*, Bryan?" asks Andrew, mockingly jocular.

"Anyway," persists Bryan manfully, not to be put off and surer (he hopes) of his facts from now on, "Bill, who is one of our old ringers, was wearing braces [suspenders], with little clips on ... "

"He's only 66," puts in Janet, for good measure.

"*And*" [Bryan speaking louder], "the rope flicked one of these clips .... It came undone. And his braces went 'PING!' over his shoulder .... Then a little while later, the other one went 'PING!'—and his trousers—slowly— descended to the ground—"

"Revealing his combinations!" adds Janet, not without a certain weakly contained glee at the memory.

"He was wearing long johns tucked into black silk socks!" Bryan confirms, heroically determined to salvage his punch line, "by which time everyone was absolutely—"

"We tried to go on with the ringing." [Janet, helplessly] .

"Bill was somewhat embarrassed by this," [Now Andrew gets a word in,] "but said, 'It's all right. Carry on.' He was worried about Janet, though, in case she was embarrassed—"

"I was the only lady in the band."

Andrew continues: "We firmly told the two boys to stop grinning and concentrate. This was their first attempt at a peal. I looked round at Richard (Bill's son), and his face was a study. He didn't know where to look ... and you *try* and concentrate for a few minutes longer ... but then you just *think* about it and you start to crack up ... and Richard started cracking up, too—"

"I'd have been all right," says Janet, "if it hadn't have been for looking at you two!"

"And it was quite obvious that we couldn't have continued with this peal. Even if we'd got to five minutes from the end, we'd still be likely to get sudden fits of the giggles ... so ... " [with a sadly hilarious sigh] "we terminated it, gently."

"And," says Janet, "we brought it round, and all stood at our bells, let go of the ropes—and then *collapsed* in *corners*."

The corner of the Saracen's Head collapsed again now, in uproarious memory of this fondly (and I suspect frequently) recounted tale. Clearly it has gone down in the annals of the Towcester Band. "Poor Bill!"

In fact, Bill didn't mind at all, or at least was sporting enough to pretend he didn't, when the event was subsequently retold in an issue of the weekly ringers' magazine, *The Ringing World.* Nor did he give up ringing. Only the next time he turned up, he was wearing braces *and* a belt. After all, a 500-year-old bell tower on a winter's night is not the warmest place in the world—physically speaking.

1988

A Matter of Resolve

Now—January 1—is the traditional time for resolutions. Or so I am told.

Personally, I made a resolution long ago, and one that is not merely yearlong in its scope, not to *make* New Year's resolutions. I have stuck to it fine.

No doubt there are those who would say this is the mark of a man who knows ahead of time that he would not keep a new resolution if he were to make one. And maybe they have a slight point—because this year, I admit I am tempted to make a fresh resolve for the coming twelve months and so (just this once) break my anti-resolution resolution.

The thing is: I twiddle my thumbs.

I have probably done it for decades. But it was only this autumn that a friend and professional colleague of mine, visiting Britain on a peripatetic assignment from the other side of the pond, well and truly alerted me to my ongoing unconscious digit-revolving propensity.

I do not do it, so far as I can tell, when driving a car. But when this friend was driving, and I was in the passenger seat, she assures me I did it quite a lot.

Even driving after dark along noisy motorways, she claims, the gentle abrasion of circumnavigating thumb against circumnavigating thumb was perfectly audible.

She wouldn't have mentioned it had it not been for the fact that I—after superhuman forbearance—made some teasing remark, aside, in company, about the noise *she* makes while driving. It was like machine-gun fire, like fireworks, like those kinds of breakfast cereal that sporadically snap, crackle, and pop in the predawn kitchen to prevent you falling asleep again over the table and drowning in the milk.

It was bubble gum.

She kept exploding orally like a turtle. *Snap! Snap!—SNAP!* Chew, chew—*snap!* Bubble gum is not all that commonplace in Britain, so I am not particularly accustomed to its native wood-notes wild. I was not irritated; but

I was somewhat in a state of continuing startlement over it.

When I finally mentioned this, she found it terribly funny. She laughed and laughed. And then she told everyone present about my audible thumb-twiddling.

Since then, I have realized I do it rather often, and my wife has started to notice it, too, and shushes me in quiet moments in theaters and concert halls. So the question is: should I make a New Year's resolution not to thumb-twiddle in 1995?

You know, I don't think I will.

I mean, is she—the one, I mean, who publicized my innocuous little pastime—is *she* going to give up percussive gummy balloon-explosions in the inter-lip region? I have heard no rumor to that effect. And why should she? If she persists in bubbling, I'll persist in twiddling. Fair's fair.

Happy New Year! Long live all bubblers and twiddlers! We all need our little differences in this era of persuasive uniformity.

1995

"Oh Wad Some Power...
the Giftie Gie Us"

He got on at South Kensington or Gloucester Road, I'm not sure which.

The London tube ride to Heathrow Airport is a long one, and I was using the time to dig deeper into a book on Bernhard Berenson. Always a fool for distraction, however, I looked up. And I couldn't prevent a grin.

Here was this man covered in paint—shoes, hair, donkey jacket, even his wristwatch, spattered and runneled with paint. He knew why I grinned and grinned back.

As soon as he opened his mouth, I knew he was Scottish. "Terrible, isn't it?" he said. "They turned the water off before we'd finished work so we couldn't wash! We're doing this painting job, you see.... That's a new watchstrap yesterday, and look at it. Terrible! Mind you, it's ma work watch.... It's just ma work watch, you know.''

Perhaps I should, at this point, have returned decisively to Berenson. But my sympathy for the Pollocked state of his watchstrap overcame my interest in Renaissance connoisseurship. And my new friend, aware of a captured ear, launched forth.

Football—a subject about which I know next to nothing—was his theme. He had prejudices (who doesn't?), and he was sticking to them. "I don't mind who I tell," he said, "and it isn't just because I'm Scottish—from Dundee as a matter of fact ... from Dundee as a matter of fact—but SCOTTISH MANAGERS are the BEST. The BEST."

The fellow sitting next to me was reading an evening paper with a banner headline: "Billy McNeill Given the Boot." And the painter's eyes happened to glance that way as he spoke. "Aye, well, I know that Aston Villa has sacked McNeill. But I say that the best manager is only as good as his players. Give a good manager a duff team, and there's nothing he can do ... nothing he can do. And I mean, if the Scottish managers aren't the best there are, why do the English keep taking them from Scotland?—that's what I say."

His logic seemed good to me (being an Englishman whose home is in Glasgow), and his way of repeating important points was persuasive. Furthermore, he backed up his contention with names: "I mean—look at Jock McSo-and-So and Archie MacThingummy, aye, and Bill Shankley, Bill Shankley."

"He was a good man,'' I agreed vigorously. (He was the only one I'd heard of; but long experience has taught me that the smallest hint of knowledge is quite enough to perpetuate a one-sided conversation.)

"A good man, aye." Encouraged by my interest, this Ancient Mariner from Dundee now proceeded to regale me with blow-by-blow accounts of most of his favorite matches. Particularly exciting were a number of graphically portrayed saves by a goalkeeper (Scottish, of course) whose elastic extensiveness and leaping wizardry are legendary, but whose name somehow escaped me.

The climax of his narrative was the game (a semifinal or something) between Dundee United and AS Roma—a highly significant contest, I gathered, in the annals of football. If Dundee United had won, it seems they would have been through to the Big Time or whatever you call international triumph and renown in the world of soccer. But alas, it was not to be. The Italian team won. "It was the referee, you see, and the linesmen. They were terrible. A duff referee and duff linesmen. They kept giving wrong decisions!" Here he paused dramatically. "Do you know what happened a year later?"

I didn't know, but it was clear he was going to tell me regardless.

He did: "A year later that referee suddenly got an enormous, brand-new house—a mansion—and two new cars. A year later, a NEW HOUSE, and TWO NEW CARS."

It seemed that the doubtful Italian victory had confirmed in my friend a bias that went far beyond football. It was *Italians* he didn't like. Not just Italians, but Italians who come to Scotland to live and work. Italians, moreover, who come to Dundee.

As he sounded forth on this pet subject, I reflected that national prejudice is a very strange thing. I didn't doubt for one moment that this congenial chatterbox would have freely enjoyed an evening's sociability with anyone of any race or creed who was a good listener. But he had never been instilled with the notion that racism is wrong. He hadn't, I'm sure, ever undergone self-questioning in this regard. He simply accepted things "the way they are,'' and that included the "fact" that all Dundee Italians are a bad lot.

Apparently there are none who escape from this infallible state of bad-lotness.

"Do you know that during the war, when the Italians sided with the Germans, the windows of the houses of all the Italians in Dundee were smashed? If their front doors were glass, they were smashed, too. The people yelled at them to come out their houses, so they could smash their windows without hurting them. No one was hurt. Just the windows smashed."

"But,"—I felt defensive—"perhaps they weren't in favor of what was happening in Italy?"

"All their windows smashed," he emphasized, as if that answered my query. "And you know what they do now? They come to Dundee, and they set up in business—ice cream, and fish and chips—and they make a fortune—and then they retire back to Italy taking all their money with them! Dundee gets nothing."

I was sure by now that no one in the carriage was missing this conversation. The man with the newspaper next to me had stopped reading and was evidently asleep—but pretending, I was certain. The pretty girl next to the garrulous painter was trying to read a book. But she kept shifting position, and I noticed that at this point she chuckled suddenly to herself. I wondered if it was the book or the conversation that amused her.

"But," I said, "I have some neighbors and friends in Glasgow who are Italian-Glaswegians. As a matter of fact, he owns a fish and chip shop. And his wife loves Italy and goes over there for most of the summer. But I believe they think of themselves as Scottish. They—and their children—have been born and educated here. They really are Glaswegians. They've certainly made a mint of money."

"Aye, and they'll retire to Italy and …." I could see this was a match I was not going to win. But at that moment the train pulled in at a station, and the girl who had chuckled stood up to disembark. She was well-dressed and moved with elegant composure. As she passed the painter, she turned to him, and, quietly and clearly, without a hint of rancor, said: "I'm from Dundee, from an Italian family." And then she walked out of the door without looking back.

As for the painter, he didn't seem to have heard her. He chatted on to me as if nothing had happened. I don't know what he was saying; all I could think of was the embarrassment I would have felt if I had been in his paint-speckled shoes. After a while I said: "Didn't she say that she was from a Dundee Italian family?"

"Aye, aye, she did," he said, "funny, that.... But it makes no difference, everything I said is true. Nobody can touch you for telling the truth...."

He considered for a second. "Aye, funny, that. Her being an Italian from Dundee."

But he wasn't fazed in the least. He prattled on to me as if I was by now an old friend, until, at last, his own station was reached. "Aye, well, here's where I've got my digs. Clean but cheap. Aye, well, good to have a chat. All the best to you." He made for the door, but then turned back. And with very loud emphasis, he pronounced: "Aye, AND LANG MAY YOUR LUM REEK!" (Translated: "Long may your chimney smoke.") Away he went again. But then he returned *again*—this time to add: "As long as it's burning someone else's coal!" And with a final conspiratorial wave, he rushed onto the platform, narrowly avoiding the closing doors.

I admit that I sighed a fairly loud sigh of relief. And as I returned to the gentler world of Lorenzo Lotto and Giorgione (as presented through the scholarship of Bernhard Berenson, that American of Lithuanian Jewish origin so long domiciled in Italy), I couldn't help wondering what my Scottish traveling companion, should he encounter some stray Italian on a tube train one day, might have to say to him about the *English*. After all, there are more than a couple of things we English have filched from his neck of the woods over the centuries, apart from football managers.

There's marmalade, for a start. Whatever Oxonians claim about this tart orange confection originating in Oxford, the fact is that it came first from Dundee.

1987

Dreams of Glorious Orbitation

I've never claimed to be Scott Zimmerman.

All the same, the world of superflight is by no means a closed book to me. Boys, after all, as Anthony Hope put it, will be boys.

Remember Frisbees? Those shocking pink UFOs that people young at heart used to launch elegantly through the air to each other—those personalized flying saucers of the beach and back street?

Well, let me assure you, those primitive little projectiles pale in comparison to the *Aerobie*. This recent invention is to Frisbees what Concorde is to the Wright Brothers' early contraption. It is not a disk, but a sleek and elegant magic ring (also, naturally, in shocking pink) and boy! it can *travel*. This is where Scott Zimmerman comes in. It was he who, on January 12, 1985, threw an Aerobie 1,046 feet in California (where else?).

His achievement is a record. It has been recognized as the *longest throw of any object in history*.

Now, frankly, such an exploit presents a challenge to anyone with an ounce of boyhood left in him, and who was I not to give it a whirl?

But the truth is that my first, and so far sole, encounter with the Aerobie contained a certain undeniable element of the ignominious. I need, it is clear, a bit more practice.

Of course, I can make excuses. The Surrey village of Cobham is hardly on a par with Pasadena spacewise, and, although the Fenester family's front lawn is Edwardian in its spaciousness and magnificent with its grassy terraces cascading down to a splendid backdrop of enormous beech and cedar trees, it does present certain hazards for wielders of The Astonishing Flying Ring.

For all I know, the Fenesters' Aerobie could be just the first of its ilk to arrive in the Old World. It was brought, as a present, by a visiting American. Apparently Aerobies are not easy to obtain even in the United States.

The Fenester children were at school, the Fenester husband at work, and we (also visitors) should have left half an hour earlier for home; Scotland takes a long while to reach by mere car.

But the thought of a couple of trial throws of that flashy aeronautical halo was irresistible. The eye-message from my wife (meaning "Now, Christopher, we haven't got time!") should have been heeded. But it wasn't.

Karen Fenester, as our excellent hostess, demonstrated the technique. She stood on the flagstones outside the front door, and, in answer to a deft wrist-flick, the Aerobie took off soaringly, landing after a fine and leisurely passage at the farthest end of the garden. A magnificent sight it was, enough to make throwers-of-discuses and putters-of-shot generally give up in despair; obviously such ancient sports, in the face of this flying wonder, have now been rendered anachronistic.

A childish excitement overtook my normally mature composure, and I charged down the garden to retrieve the volitational nimbus and return it to sender. I would guess the extent of the Fenester front lawn approaches 100 yards. The booklet about the Aerobie's virtues and uses declares that most people can throw an Aerobie 100 to 200 yards with surprising ease.

Well, it hurts me to admit this, but my own first attempt was decidedly middling: the Aerobie veered to the left and came to earth far too soon.

We could hardly head for Scotland with such an anticlimax hanging over us. Reputations count for *something*. "Right," the kid in me shouted, "one more go, and that's it!" My wife's look indicated even less time than before. But it was tame compared with her face when what was about to occur, occurred.

With supreme determination, I swept the Saturnian circle of dazzling carmine—molded in the USA from premium materials to exacting quality standards—upward and outward. I aimed for outer space, for apogee, for resistless, perpetual motion. The theme music from *Chariots of Fire* sounded; the cameras whirred in very slow motion. The Aerobie lifted, lifted, sped away, swung to the left, magnificent, sublime—and then (like Winnie the Pooh into his gorse-bush) it flew gracefully into a very large cedar tree. And there, visible only from certain carefully selected angles, it came to rest. It was, in a word, *stuck*.

Thus it is that the little ironies of experience modify our ambitions. Now, instead of dreams of glorious orbitation (and if there isn't such a word, there should be), all that concerned me was getting The Ring down to earth again—though, frankly, this seemed somewhat less attainable than licking Mr. Zimmerman's record. The Ring did look quite remarkably—well, in a word, *stuck*. Stuck is what it looked. Self-evidently, storm or tempest was not going to dislodge it; and anyway the family would be returning at the end of the day, eager for aerobatics, and not at all planning to spend the evening climbing trees. Something had to be done!

Cedar trees, Lebanese or not, are known for the generous spread of their branches. The Ring was at least 15 feet up, and no ladder, had one been in the vicinity, would have reached it; it was so far out from the trunk. A branch strong enough to hold an Aerobie is not necessarily ladderworthy. Shaking the lower branches proved useless. Needles fell in my mouth, but no Aerobie.

Then Karen produced her son's football. It needed blowing up, but no matter. The principle was classical: if you lose a ball, you send another to the same place, and you find them both. Unfortunately, there can be a catch to this proverbial procedure. This catch was very soon demonstrated.

I grasped the inflated football. After one throw had almost, but not quite, dislodged the irresponsible Ring, and after another throw had made the ball simply disappear in the luxuriance of brambles at the tree's feet, I felt that the third throw must surely be destined for triumphant success. I threw with might and main and sound effects, and the football—joined the Aerobie. There it was in the tree fraternally aloft, chummily stuck. It looked down at us as if, Cheshire Cat-like, it was *all smile*. It gloated.

By this time, wives were champing. Embarrassment was mounting. Ideas were running short. We were all sort of laughing a lot.

"How about this?" asked Karen suddenly, pointing to a fallen branch on the ground.

"Far too heavy," I said, giggling gloomily. But, in fact, it was lighter than I imagined.

A rescue, of course, should be heroic. I did my best to indicate by groans and grunts that it was a positively Herculean effort to lift that sturdy branch above my head and tickle the objects on high. In truth it all proved easy enough, and the next moment the ball fell out of the tree, followed by the Aerobie.

But the dramatics paid off. A loud cheer went up from the assembled spectators. It was a good moment.

The Zimmerman standard may not have been reached—but I bet I'm the first forty-plus boy in history to get an Aerobie AND a football stuck on the same branch of a cedar tree in Surrey, England, and then manage to *get them both down again*.

Achievements come in all sizes.

1985

Don't Bank on It

There's a bank in Scotland that makes its clerks bear on their sweaters the slogan "A Friend for Life." I have little direct experience of that particular bank, yet I find its motto somehow unconvincing.

Banks have never struck me as especially friendly places, though "for life" does seem rather apt. Once one starts a relationship with a bank, it does tend toward continuance. Actually, I suspect that the notion of a "friendly" bank, and thus of a "friendly bank manager," may be several hundred percent less credible than that, say, of a "friendly policeman." At least with the latter, you have no reason to feel guilty so long as you haven't committed a crime.

But with bank managers you never seem to feel entirely innocent, even when you are. Something about them, and it's not just their eyebrows, puts you at a disadvantage. They have that kind of unbudging sense of rightness that belongs to those who know they have more of what you have less of. It's summed up in a parallel drawn by Peter De Vries between Ivy League schools and banks: "They," he wrote, "will give you an education the way the banks will give you money—provided you can prove to their satisfaction that you don't need it."

Which is why I was rather pleased recently to find myself momentarily with a branch of my bank (not a Scottish one) eating meekly out of my hand.

To protect the guilty, I will call her Mrs. Wappensoup—though this pseudonym isn't half as unusual as her real name. I first met Mrs. Wappensoup—she is a very nice person—when I was applying for some Italian lire. Lire come by the thousands. Perhaps it was this that confused her. Anyway, about three hours after I returned home, Mrs. Wappensoup was on the phone. "Could you kindly count the lire I gave you this morning?" she said, pleadingly. I did. "Ah, it's as I thought," she groaned. "I gave you far too much. Is there some way in which you could return the extra to us?" It was a richly novel experience, this. A bank had been overgenerous to me! It wanted its lire back, of course, but the temporary possession of them gave me a fine feeling of tables turned. The bank was to close within the hour.

"Well," I said nonchalantly, "I suppose that I could come into town again. A book's just come in for me at Smith's. I might perhaps get a taxi and maybe drop the money off on the way ... if there's time.... "

Mrs. Wappensoup seemed a little comforted. Extraordinarily, the taxi driver was also called Wappensoup—though he assured me he had no relative in a bank; he only wished he had. By now the bank was shut to the ordinary public, but since it so eagerly wanted what I had, it elaborately, and with remarkable grace, I felt, unbolted the heavy doors specially for me. No bank has ever shown such pleasure to see me before.

I have encountered Mrs. Wappensoup frequently since—asking, in fact, for such a variety of different foreign bank notes over the last couple of years that now she always greets me with "Oh, yes—and where are we off to this time?" She refuses to believe these trips are work. "Oh, yes," she says incredulously. "That's *your* story."

Occasionally, I remind her of the time she gave me too much—just to keep her on her toes.

And then last week, I was in the bank once more, this time to buy some Dutch guilders. I was served by a young man I'd never seen before. As he checked the exchange rate, Mrs. Wappensoup came by. To me she said, "You're not off *again*?" And to him, as she pulled a strip of receipts from his till and studied them, she sighed loudly and commented, "Now what've you done? What a mess!"

The young man looked at me quizzically. "She's always getting at me," he said.

"Only because he deserves it," she interrupted briskly. "He writes *stories* all over this—look!" The receipts were scrawled with handwritten corrections. They both laughed.

"If she gets too bossy and stroppy," I said to the young man, "just ask her about the time she gave me too many lire!"

"I don't believe it! She didn't!"

Mrs. Wappensoup laughed and admitted it, and as the young man carefully counted out my guilders, he couldn't stop a smile spreading all over his face.

And what happened three hours later?

Another phone call. *This* time from the young man. Very downcast. "You're never going to believe this ... " he began.

"You *haven't*," I said.

"I think so," he said.

I counted the guilders while he waited on the phone. There were fifty too many. "You have!" I said.

"Yes," he said, "and I thought it was impossible."

"Well, I can't come rushing in with it today," I said, with a touch of absolute glee, "and I'm off to the Netherlands first thing in the morning."

"Just put it in the post then."

"And who is responsible if the post office loses it?"

"I am," he replied morosely.

It turned out that I managed to drive past the bank late that evening. Into the envelope with the money, I also slipped a postcard of one of my favorite pieces of ancient sculpture from Glasgow's Burrell Collection. It is a terra cotta of a lion head of the Isin-Larsa period. Whoever made this goofy-looking lion mask with its braided beard, comic ears, crew cut, contour-line mustachios, beady eyes, and enormous gaping mouth, presumably imagined he was expressing the most awe-inspiring ferocity. He wasn't. His efforts fell flat. His lion head is dafter than Dopey.

What I wrote on the back of this card was unlike anything I have ever written to a bank before: "Here's your money! The face on the front says it all. Best wishes."

Friend for Life? Come to think of it, maybe I have made a couple of lifelong friends in a bank after all.

1988

Columns in Mercurial Moonlight

It is characteristic of Greece, it seems: one minute, humanity is so pressing and noisy that you wonder how such an apparently chaotic country can survive its overpopulation. And the next minute, you find yourselves in a place devoid of any other inhabitants whatsoever—a cat or three maybe, but otherwise nothing but the night air and us.

That's the way it was our first evening in Athens. We had gone for a stroll, and, after a while, we had climbed so far from the pedestrian street bursting with light and life that now, down there, it appeared to belong to another world. Its cafes, nut sellers, puppeteers, and souvenir shops—its mayhem of people like a fury of summer bees desperately searching for hives—might even belong to a different time.

High in the silence loomed a gigantic wall—a dark and sheer masonry towering above us. It was not easy to ignore. What on earth could such a bastion surround? Barracks? A prison?

"Could it be the Acropolis?" my wife hazarded.

"Oh, no, no!" exclaimed I. Now why do people like me, in places they have never before visited, speak with such authority? "No, that's over on the other side of the city," I said, gesturing with sweeping emphasis. "I looked at the map."

Maybe I did. But the fact is that David Livingstone and I are not quite like two peas in a pod. His burning dedication to mapping a continent, to comprehending vast river systems, to meeting unexpected travelers in remote places, is not exactly my scene. (Though I believe the explorer did not always get the sources of his rivers right.)

To put it another way, I admit that my sense of direction really isn't anything to write home about. I am not a born traveler. I cling to a persistently discombobulating confusion about the difference between east and west (north and south I just about manage). Typically, that first evening in Athens only served to underline, yet again, my habitual geographical incompetence.

We strolled on, the wall overshadowing our amble. After a while we glimpsed—peeping over the wall-cliff's lowering, curved silhouette—part of a pediment and a procession of classical columns standing floodlit in gold. There was something quite magical about them, as if they had been conjured out of a vast top hat. More columns appeared as we walked. Then the floodlight flickered, went out, came on again, and then was finally extinguished.

We could still see the columns, even though everything was now reduced to dark grays, softly intense blacks, and that strangely potent, but just-perceptible commodity, the wizardry of mercurial moonlight.

Suddenly we felt deeply enclosed in the stuff of memory.

What we were gazing at was, of course, the Acropolis—though I was still slow to admit it. After all, the world is encircled with classical columns from Washington to Delhi. The classical column is everywhere. It survives all change, resurfaces in all periods, and dignifies churches, town halls, colleges, and fish-and-chip shops. It adapts with rectitude even to the most crass architectural misuse.

But it was the Greeks who started it—or at least refined in stone what must primitively have been mere tree trunks to claim columns as architectural archetypes, forever Greek. But when you are actually in Greece, it takes a while for it to sink in that here, on this very ground, rest classical columns as they were originally conceived. Here they were invented. That night, I stared at the columns above the wall, and all I thought was—columns.

Then, at last, astonishment dawned: we (or I, in my complete conviction that it was in another part of town) had managed to come upon the Acropolis *by mistake*!

Livingstone knew when he was approaching the Victoria Falls. Indeed, he set out deliberately to see them. He was the first white man to do so, but not at all the first man. He wasn't disappointed, of course; he lay face downward, overwhelmed. It was a sight to be seen "by angels in their flight."

But just suppose he had come upon the falls unexpectedly! Our difficulty today is *familiarity*. I recall an English friend taken to see Niagara Falls and other remarkable places in America on her first visit. She enjoyed it. But she kept saying: "It's just like Johnny Morris. I saw that on Johnny Morris." This British TV personality had recently made a documentary about travel in the States. To a degree, he had preempted, and unwittingly diluted, the freshness of this visitor's experiences.

This happens too much in our period. If only we could sidle up to the Mona Lisa in the Louvre and catch her off her guard, not quite smiling. Or suddenly spot the Leaning Tower of Pisa from a passing bus and feel worried about it keeling over. If only we could not know about everything before we *see* it.

That first encounter of ours with the Acropolis (later to be seen conventionally in broad daylight with a million other tourists) was almost of this order. There we were, treading, in increasing awe, the large shiny stones of the pathways below the Acropolis. These stones have been smoothed by countless touristic feet. Yet that night there wasn't another tourist anywhere near. The mobile shop, which was set up in an open space and in daylight did a rattling trade in fresh orange juice, looked as if it had been abandoned for centuries.

Up the glistening stones we meandered, careful not to slip—can you slip on moonlight?—and above us the Parthenon, grandly in view now, and then quite suddenly below us, dropping away from our feet, the great scoop of a stone amphitheater. I breathed in. It was like being the first people on earth to be here.

1992

VI.
Important People

Hand It to Her Majesty

I have decided, after considerable ponderment, lasting a couple of minutes at least, that I will not, after all, have my portrait painted.

Or not by Antony Williams, anyway.

It strikes me that non-royal-watchers may be (as I was) unfamiliar with this portrait painter's name. Suffice it to explain, then, that he is the chap who recently did the face of Her Majesty Queen Elizabeth—though it was not the face that was the problem.

It was the hands.

They do not look (as delineated by Mr. Williams with an extraordinary degree of realism) at all like the hands to which a queen might judiciously lay claim. Instead, they contain, as the *Times* (of *London*—naturally) has put on record, "the uncompromising detail of broken fingernails."

One might not mind if such fingers were well-gloved (as I am led to believe they generally are, though perhaps not when she washes the dishes); then they might be just about OK for the occasional shaking. But they are not the sort of hands with which you would willingly be knighted or anything like that.

Britain sports one or two professional royal watchers, people with superior accents on whom the news media call when they want a vivid opinion on the latest royal happening. Lord St. John of Fawsley (he is not pronounced "Saint John" incidentally, but "Sinjun") is unquestionably the cherry on top of this particular cake, the royal pronouncer-in-chief.

Whenever he has anything to pronounce of a royal nature, he does so with a well-oiled assurance that convinces his listeners that he has, since birth, known Her Majesty like the back of his hand, and on this occasion, he "declared emphatically" (said the *Times*): "These are not the hands of the Queen."

The very next day, however, the artist no less emphatically counter-declared: "These *are* the hands of the Queen." Things were getting dangerously close to pantomime.

Without wishing to be picky, an art critic might point out here that neither of them was right. They were, to be strictly accurate, not hands at all, but a painter's *depiction* of hands, which is another matter altogether.

The Queen, as is her wont, has said nothing on the subject—or for that matter about her various subjects who seem to know her better than she knows herself. Whatever your nails are like, I do not think it can be easy being the Queen. I mean, her habitual, dignified silence is all very well, but isn't she ever *tempted* to end needless speculation by making a simple announcement on a given matter?

If these are "her hands," then wouldn't it be better to say, in a good round royal way, that friend Sinjun has taken his loyalty to her person rather too far this time? Or contrariwise, if Williams has painted someone else's manual and digital regions and perpetrated them on the Queen (which is certainly what the old portrait painters did), wouldn't a swift, firm denial from Buckingham Palace be in order? Something along the line of: "The Queen would like it to be known that she does not now have, and never has had, a broken fingernail." That would do the trick. And Sinjun could smile smugly.

It is in the fingernail department that I myself would most prefer non-portrayal. In fact, I can't help wondering if the Queen has perhaps been digging a hole in her basement lately. I have. And I can tell you, it plays havoc with things cuticular. This is only a theory on my part, of course, but it might be a reasonable, and not I hope a treasonable, explanation.

Although I believe Her Majesty may not herself be stunningly tall, the Duke of Edinburgh, I seem to remember from when I met him, was quite a height above sea level; and if their place is anything like ours, walking along the back passage in their basement may well be impossible to do without inadvertently crowning one's royal noggin on any number of joists and hot water pipes.

So it may have dawned on their majesties that a bit of do-it-yourself was in order—a touch of the pick-and-shovel technique, a bucketing-out of earth—in order to lower the floor of said passage accordingly. That, anyway, is why *I* am digging a hole in *our* passage here at No. 48, and if the Queen and Duke have not launched on a similar project of late, then I for one will be quite taken aback. The Duke is rather busy, I know, with this and that—watching polo matches and so forth—so it has probably fallen to the Queen to do the actual digging business.

Now you may well ask why she has not been wearing heavy-duty workman's gloves while she grubs and grovels away at the subsoil among her foundations. Again, I can only guess, but I suspect this is because she is so fed up with wearing gloves all day that when she goes down there for a spell of happy excavation (filling an odd half hour just after *Coronation Street,* probably) she simply prefers the feeling of mother earth right between the royal fingers to the clammy, intervening enclosure of yet more gloves.

Down there in the musty darkness, she can just be herself, clawing away at the geological strata, not a care in the world, humming, "Dig-dig, Dig-dig, Dig-dig, Dig-dig" to her heart's content and without a thought of asking Disney about copyright. She couldn't do that at a state dinner, I'll be bound. No way.

But what I would like to know is *when* did Sinjun last authentically and face-to-face have a look at Her Majesty's fingernails? Does he just pop into the palace when he feels like it and demand a peek? And how can he be so positive that she has not been spending her spare time having a jolly good dig at the basement floor since he last had audience with her?

The *Times* went on to say that "Lord St. John ... granted that it was a powerful painting. 'But it has not got the essence of the Queen, which is her serenity, benevolence and happiness. It has caught one aspect of her, but a portrait should capture the whole person.'" Is his meaning that you can't be happy and serene and also have a broken fingernail?

It must be wonderful to be so sure about everything, so persistently, so confidently right; to voice your opinion with such incontrovertible self-assurance; to know everything there is to know about Queens and portrait painting and portrait painting and Queens. Wonderful.

But I'd bet (if I were a betting man) that Sinjun has never in his life dug a hole in a basement. You can tell just by looking at his shining morning face that *his* fingernails are immaculate.

1996

Sir Alec Is Everywhere

There is a story the British comedian Arthur Askey told. In a lift (English for "elevator") in a Blackpool hotel, another man said to him: "Has anyone ever told you you look like Arthur Askey?"

He admitted undemonstratively that some people had mentioned it.

Next day, the same two men met again in the same lift.

"Do you know," said the first, "I've discovered that Arthur Askey is actually appearing in Blackpool just now!"

The renowned comedian thought he really should now admit who he was. "Well, you see, actually, I *am* Arthur Askey."

The man looked at him with a knowing grin. "I bet you wish you were!" he said.

It is not easy, I imagine, having a famous face. Or even one that looks like a famous person's face. At one time, I kept seeing Meryl Streep everywhere. Not the real Meryl—at least I think not. Just a large number of women who looked exactly like her—coming down the aisle in Tesco's, queuing for stamps, and shoving plastic cards into bank machines—things of that sort.

It is odd, though. Not all superstars have been granted such ubiquity. I never, for instance, saw Norma Jean repetitively cloned—except as painted and silk-screened by Andy Warhol. (And Warhol himself I saw only once, in Texas—or was it that chap who impersonated him?)

Nor do I think, for example, that Audrey Hepburn's doe eyes and sapling neck were remotely imitable—though there was a woman behind the counter in the charity shop the other week who claimed she had, when younger, done her best to copy the Hepburn look. At the time, I was looking at a calendar devoted to the star, and while I credited the charitable lady's ambition, I privately doubted the achievement.

It has been a while now, in fact, since I spotted the redoubtable Streep on all sides.

These days, it is Sir Alec Guinness I keep spotting.

I see him—double—quite frequently on Sunday mornings. He is two brothers who are piously headed churchward down the hill toward Partick. The spitting image of Guinness the both of them. Twins, I suppose. Or maybe triplets?

Sir Alec is one of those actors whose appearance disappears into a character. So it is paradoxical that other people should look like him, unless everyone does. Perhaps it is a case of the more he tries to vanish, the more noticeable he inadvertently becomes.

His newest burst into book form, a published diary, has him pictured on the back and front covers as John Le Carré's George Smiley. He told his publisher that he hates having his photograph taken—a strange reticence in a professional actor who has appeared in countless films—so they had to make do with a photo of him playing a character. The telling point is, though, that the photographs are instantly identifiable as Guinness.

His book, incidentally, is wittily titled *My Name Escapes Me: The Diary of a Retiring Actor.* Two recent events he describes (last entry June 6, 1996) touch on the question of recognition.

One took place when he had received "an invitation to dine at the Admiralty" (sounds like Samuel Pepys), "and a fine and marvellous occasion it was.... "

"When I arrived," he writes, "the Flag Lieutenant (for it was he) greeted me with 'So glad to see you!' and what I took to be a pleased smile of recognition.

"He invited me to see where I would be sitting. 'You are here,' he said, 'with Mr. So-and-so on one side and Admiral So-and-so on the other. Opposite you, Alec Guinness, the actor.'

"'Ah!' I said, "a 'Doppelganger!' But he didn't get it."

The other story is entered on "Tuesday 21 February" (1995) and reads thus: "Today I have picked up a rather good notice in an American film trade paper for a performance I have never given in a film I have never heard of. It says that I am 'almost unrecognizable' in the film. I like the 'almost.'"

I, on the other hand, have no difficulty recognizing Sir Alec's manifestation every morning in the park near here in Glasgow. (He does well to get here so early. He lives in London.)

It is what Le Carré (in his revealing introduction to the book) describes as Guinness's "fluid face" that gives him away. Here he is daily, jogging. I am dog-walking, but Sir Alec, though a known dog lover, ventures forth dogless: another tactic, I suppose, to hide his identity.

Until today, he seems to have been somewhat dour and monosyllabic in response to my suggestion that it's a good morning. Perhaps he is taken by surprise that anyone might have the temerity to address him. (Probably it is the desire for anonymity felt by most famous people, which is almost as keen as the dismay they experience when nobody spots them.)

The most he has hitherto managed in reply is a profoundly Scottish-Irish "G-morrnin', surr!" and he's quickly gone on his way. (The accent is also clearly one of the actor's ingenious chameleon-esque devices.)

But this morning, I almost had a conversation with him.

"Good morning," I said. "A lovely one."

"That it is, surr," he replied, slightly slowing his pace. "That it is." And he very nearly smiled.

"Though rather chilly," I ventured.

"It is indeed; it is indeed!" And he smiled quite broadly. "You haf t' kape moovin'."

This, I think, is progress. Soon we may be discussing ozone depletion at length or abstruse forms of animatronics—who can tell? Perhaps he can even give me a few tips on acting.

Though there is one thing I will *never* do, no matter how chummy we become. I will never blow his cover. That would not be fair. We all have a right to our privacy.

1996

Boulez in a Taxi

If I'd known then what I know now, would I have let him—and his two colleagues, whoever they were—ride in my taxi?

Well, probably. Yes. The thing is, most of us ordinary types are suckers for reputation, "greatness," and even notoriety. Few of us object to the idea of rubbing shoulders—even if only in the form of a doorway collision—with the famous.

For them, it must be a mixed blessing to have a recognizable face. But for the rest of us, it's a staggering moment, a story to tell.

One of the pleasures of attending the annual International Festival of the Arts in Edinburgh is that if you do not see at least half a dozen figures of stage, film, music, art, or stand-up comedy walking down the street, sitting in an audience, or having a meal, then you feel cheated. It is one of the side benefits of festival going, a partial compensation for the ever-rising cost of tickets.

In 1998, for the third year running, a "Festival Lecture" has been given under Edinburgh University's sponsorship. I went to the first (by George Steiner) but missed the second (by Peter Stein).

Standing now outside my hotel on the opposite side of town, I was getting a little concerned that although I had a ticket for this year's lecture, I might miss it also—because the taxi I'd ordered had not arrived.

As I waited, three men emerged from the hotel behind me. They asked the doorman how quickly they could get a taxi. They were obviously late and concerned.

Then I recognized one of them. Not so many years ago, I would have retreated at this point into a shell of snail-like embarrassment and pretended nonentity. But today, for whatever reason, an awful couldn't-care-less sort of boldness took hold of me. I turned and offered to share my taxi with them.

The thing is, I knew they were going my way. I knew they would be at the lecture.

After a moment's hesitation, they also shrugged away caution and decided, on inspection, that I perhaps was not all that dangerous, and that a taxi (imminently) in the hand was probably worth two in the bush. So they said, "Yes, thanks."

The taxi came.

Pierre Boulez got in first. He was eager to get moving. It doesn't do for the lecturer to arrive too late for his own lecture. His two colleagues and I followed. A polite argument did not deter Mr. Boulez from sitting on the jump seat, with his back to the driver. "How far is it?" the great composer asked.

"Oh, about ten minutes or less," I said.

And then there followed a long silence.

The taxi lurched and swung over cobbled back streets and around steep Scottish corners. What on earth does one say to a legend whose work has been discussed in books and concert programs for decades? To one who is ensconced firmly in the pantheon with Stravinsky, Berg, Bartók, Schönberg, and Cage? What does one *dare* say, especially if the legend himself is not saying a lot, and especially if one's knowledge of modern (or any kind of) classical music is deficient to the point of sadness?

I mean, I wasn't about to introduce the subject of atonality or serialism and ask whether he agreed that music writer Paul Griffiths was accurate in his description of the "two kinds of music" in Boulez's work *Sur Incises*:

"... a rapid toccata-style mobility marked by stutterings of immediate note repetition, and strummings at the bottom of the keyboard."

I couldn't mention this casually just then, partly because it's difficult to memorize, and partly because it was printed in the program for the concert I was going to hear that evening—and I hadn't read it yet.

To travel in a taxi with the stellar may be a cosmic event (for you, if not for him); but I began to feel that if it were to take place from start to finish in *blank soundlessness*, it would, perhaps, achieve only a rather low degree of memorability.

And then, fortunately, Boulez spoke.

"Going backward," he observed, "you almost feel you are on the right side of the road."

The American (as one of his companions turned out to be) who was sitting on my right and facing the maestro said: "You can see for the first time where you have been."

"I once tried driving in Britain," Boulez bouled on, "but I didn't trust myself." Then the conductor, renowned for his exacting attention to detail and for driving his musicians to relentless levels of concentration, admitted that if his attention had lapsed while driving on the left, who knows what might have happened?

After this opening salvo, conversation went along comfortably and amusingly. I thanked him for the fine concert he'd conducted the night before. (I had been there, so this was a comparatively safe topic.) And we all agreed that though the hall could have been fuller, the audience could hardly have been more enthusiastic.

Boulez in the taxi seemed, I thought, philosophical about the difficulty of filling concert halls for modern music.

But in his lecture, he made it clear that he is *not* resigned to diminishing audiences. He advocates more audience-friendliness, far more flexibility on all sides, and modern concert halls where both audience and musicians can be easily rearranged. He favors an escape from the format of 19th-century concert halls, still the model for many architects at the end of the 20th; he wants smaller orchestras, more varied in type; he proposes more education about modern music for both adults and children.

He admitted that in the early days, he and his fellow modernists did not care enough about their work and intentions being understood. Today, he, at least, is working hard to counter that indifference. He described his evolving "Cité de la Musique" ("City of Music") in Paris, showing how this center puts his pedagogic and popularizing ideals into practice. (It even has a host of local children playing Balinese gamelan instruments.) His aim is that "people will have no fear" of music.

At the end of his lecture, the audience applauded vigorously.

The critics, however, did not let us forget that this kindly-faced septuagenarian was once a gadfly in the music world. Earlier photos of him hint at his spikiness. He even, we are informed, once provoked everyone by advocating the destruction by dynamite of all opera houses.

One critic pointed out that Boulez's campaign today for making classical music, old or new, more accessible is paradoxically at odds with his own music. This, the critic contends, makes no concessions to populism.

But that night, after the lecture, I found myself in an Edinburgh concert hall listening to Boulez's *Sur Incises* (the latest development of a work begun in 1994 and still open to more or less endless expansion). And I enjoyed the music's openness; its interplay of pause and conversation, of the sporadic and the continuous; and its extreme contrasts between unexpected, explosive bursts and degrees of strange delicacy. It was like a series of stones being tossed with a splash into a river of silence, each time sending out shock waves and ripples of music.

Is it music? Oh, yes, it's music.

Is it uncompromising, difficult, disturbing? Could be. But that is the way art should be, n'est-ce pas?

And now for the burning question. *Would I invite a man who wants to blow up opera houses to share my taxi again?* Yes I would, decidedly. Because now I am all primed with things I want to ask him.

1998

Maestro

**Orchestral conductors are enormously intriguing creatures—
especially, I suspect, to those of us once described by a long-standing
music critic as "unschooled listeners."** Such noncognoscenti are not all that
rare, truth to tell, and we are mainly responsible, surely, for turning
conductors into stars.

At the close of some favorite symphony or other, we tend to direct all our
vast enthusiasm at that bowing maestro on the podium. The composer is
forgotten. The orchestra is barely given a glance. After all, the conductor
looks so much *warmer* than any of the players.

The conductor is the master painter; the musicians are his or her dabs of
paint. Through him the music comes; by him it is evoked. His antics do far
more than make the beat plain to the orchestra or alert the patiently waiting
(but slightly dozing) celesta player.

They are also a deliberate means of communication with the entire hall.
From the back, no less than from the front, the swelling tensions of a piece,
its meticulous precisions, its sudden and exacting needs for *pianissimi* or
fortissimi, its grand abandonment, its breadth of exultation, are all visibly
expressed by the conductor.

To the sound itself (for which he takes such credit), the conductor adds the
italics and punctuation of gesture, of strained arms, of startling tautness of the
shoulders—of brisk nod, of hands flung apart in some wild appeal to the
universe. If you shut your eyes during such a performance, it's certain that
something of the quality of the sound will be missed. Or that's what we
believe at the time.

In an Edinburgh concert hall the other week, we watched a French
conductor take his orchestra through the paces of a long stretch of ballet
music. As if self-conscious about the missing element of the dance itself, this
nimble-fingered, acrobatically inclined musical director saw to it that his
own one-man performance came as near to the choreographic as possible.

The reverse philosophy was practiced at a later concert by Daniel

131

Barenboim. The piece was the *Boléro* by Ravel, a work of self-perpetuating motion that unwinds like a spring. Through most of it, the conductor stood stock still. Such an unusual posture had its own electrifying effect.

There is showmanship in conducting, of course, and it is not easy for the unknowledgeable to guess when the performance is a response to the music and when it genuinely inspires it. Perhaps the line is better left blurry. The creative and the appreciative are two sides of the same act when it comes to art-making.

But the role of the conductor remains mysterious. In other kinetic art forms, the director is generally invisible by the time the performance takes place. Even prompters, in the theater, are hidden. The conductor's function, however, embraces not just rehearsal, but also performance.

The adopted word "conductor" itself is suggestive. The ideal orchestral conductor combines traits from other familiar uses of the same name. He is not all musician; he is also part bus conductor and part lightning conductor. The first believes himself in charge of a moving vehicle and dutifully hurries people off and onto it at designated intervals. The second is a kind of medium for conveying to earth a vivid, elemental, and even potentially dangerous force. It is this balance of practical organization and fire-dazzle that marks the visible art of orchestral conductors.

There is little doubt that an orchestra can be subtly or brilliantly transformed by a conductor. Barbirolli, in January 1966, conducted his "dear Berlin lads" (the Berlin Philharmonic) playing Beethoven's *Eroica* (not for the first time). A German critic described it as "a near-ideal balance of tension, intelligence, and emotion. The orchestra was brought to life by Sir John.... One could hardly believe it was the same orchestra which recently played this work so particularly badly...."

In fact, as Michael Kennedy's biography of Barbirolli movingly shows, the relationship between the great orchestra's musicians and the conductor was one of extraordinary tenderness and regard. He called their playing "all so beautiful and so generous." *They* ranked him "among the exceptional, really musical, conductors."

Kennedy writes that his rehearsals were "never dull. Humor, anger, white-hot interest, petulant slaps at the score or radiant joy—any of these might be forthcoming." He was endlessly thorough in preparation of a concert, and then, in the evening, he was able to "inspire the players afresh and to make all his carefully marked detail sound spontaneous."

And the audiences—in Barbirolli's case, they were not unknown to give him ovations lasting longer than half an hour. They even refused to leave when the hall lights were put out. Where precisely did the magic lie? His face and hands, we are told, "could have coaxed music from a slab of concrete." His baton was a "wand." He "had indefinable power of communication." He was even said to have "thought sound."

But the really telling word of explanation, I think, is to be found in a sharp remark he once fired at a string player "in whom," Kennedy writes, "he suspected a lack of intensity in Schubert's ... C Major Symphony."

"If," said Barbirolli, "you don't *love* to play this music, you should go out and chop wood." The italics were his.

1985

VII.
Children Seen and Heard

Slow-Time Kid

When it comes to things musical—or just things in general—I've never really thought of myself as a devotee of "slow time," to borrow Keats's measured phrase. Those deep and ponderous passages often seem to me mere groundswell, as a kind of mumbled preparation for the glories of a fast and furious climax. This is a vulgar failing on my part, doubtless—a lack of high and solemn seriousness—but one whose tar not a few of us are brushed with, I suspect. Yes, I'm a con brio and con fuoco creature, if not positively a con delirio one: lentamente is for the snails.... And yet ...

The brilliant and breathless are such commonplaces of our century: the race is to the swift—the hare trounces the tortoise—they don't "serve who only stand and wait"—not nowadays. In the eyes of the up-to-date, there is no deadlier sin than Delay.... And yet ...

Talking of delay, my wife and I were traveling by London Underground train a week or two ago. We were on holiday, officially, but may well have been in a hurry all the same. I don't remember.

But what I do remember is a tiny child and her young mother in the compartment. This child had hit, with total unselfconsciousness (and that's a quality to keep), on the essence of "slow time."

She was eating an ice cream cone. Well, no, she wasn't exactly eating it: she was relishing and reveling in it. She was (almost literally) absorbed in it. But her pleasure was, at the same time, oddly absentminded. Above all, it was without the slightest hint of haste.

Gradually, the attention of everyone near this infant turned toward her; but the infant herself had no idea at all that anyone anywhere was watching her.

An ice cream, of course, is par excellence the hastiest of pleasures: now you see it—now you don't. Almost before it is paid for, it must be licked into shape. Quickly or it'll melt! "At my back I always hear/time's winged chariot hurrying near...."

Leicester Square, Tottenham Court Road, Goodge Street ... Euston; the train shot through its tunnels, doors opened and shut, passengers rushed on and off—Mornington Crescent, Camden Town.... Regardless of all this motion and commotion, the possessor of the ice cream sat in her push-chair blissfully undisturbed, taking a very occasional and a ve-ry small taste of it ve-ry slow-ly—just now and then—on her tongue. Inevitably the dollop of ice started to collapse, the warm runny cream melted into the paper wrapped round the wafer cone (by now soggy with wear and tear) and ran over the child's hands and down her front.

Adults can mysteriously adore in babies what they wouldn't for a moment tolerate in older children. This glorious mess prompted nothing but smiles, and her mother (now attempting to clean her up a little) was clearly immensely proud of all this admiration.

If that baby of hers could have known the poetry of Andrew Marvell, this would have been the moment for her to suddenly look up and announce to her captivated audience: "Yonder all before us lie deserts of vast eternity."

The poet meant these words as an incentive to speed. But they could, I feel, also mean just the opposite: "So what's all the hurry?" Certainly this child, this prodigy of slow motion, would have taken his words that way. She had introduced into that hive of haste a profound gradualism. At two years old, she had understood something deeply true, and something deeply funny, about "slow time."

Perhaps, after all, there is something to be said for the pace of snails.
1981

Wake Up, You!

One might say that getting up in the morning is not exactly one's forte. It is not, I find, something to be attempted without gentle encouragement.

But most of the various up-getting techniques and technologies seem to involve a degree of unkindness. Alarm clocks by your ear that rattle you rigid. Alarm clocks afar that don't stop until you get up and stop them. Alarm clocks that are so enthusiastic that their internal vibrations start building up to the morning siren the night before and never let you get to sleep in the first place. Early morning calls from the telephone people, doubly shaming because *another person* is let into the awful secret that you are Not at Your Best First Thing—and because you have to pay for the privilege.

Then there are bantam cockerels. Very effective getter-uppers. I had one who managed to evoke from me all kinds of ghastly denials after only crowing *once*. When sadly this splendiferous tyrant shuffled off to (possibly) happier haunting grounds, his widowed hen turned into his surrogate. You've never heard of a bantam *hen* crowing? Well, you have now. And let me assure you that to be vocalized out of bed by a cockerel is humiliating enough; to be roused by a crowing hen—well, it's crushing. As Ken the farmer puts it: "A whistling woman and a crowing hen/Are no good for God or men." (You don't expect political correctness from a Yorkshire farmer AD 1974.)

Just now, however, I am away from home staying with friends, and I am being subjected to a new trial technique for getting up. I don't quite know what to make of it. No cocks, no clocks—just a *very* small, very bright-eyed, pip-nosed little girl.

Her name, neatly enough, is Tamsin. She LOVES waking people up.

First, she clicks the door handle up and down a large number of times. It ricochets through my soft, deep dreams like shot peas. It goes on until Tamsin is satisfied.

Next comes the opening of the door. This can happen several times, in and out and in, until I make it clear that I have noticed.

Then she fetches a large mug of hot orange juice and marches round to the bedside table with it.

"Drink it," she commands.

And when I just shut my eyes, she says, a little louder, "DRINK IT!"

Then she goes to the corner of what after all is her room (she's sleeping with her parents for the duration) and picks up a cone of vari-colored plastic rings on a stick.

Carrying this over, she sits on me (funny man: he groans if you sit on him). And like a true artist, undeterred by the lack of encouragement from those present or the world at large, she proceeds to give me an Advanced Examination on How to Play with the Toy.

"Which color is on top then?" (Very sharp voice).

"O-oh," (groan), "er—pink."

"It's yellow."

"Yes—yellow."

"What color is the biggest?" "Where is it?" "How do they come off?" "How do they go on again?" "Are they all different?" "Can't you do it?" "Look—it's EASY!" "You do it."

Elizabethan torture in the Tower, Solzhenitzen's camp interrogations, and ancient Chinese water drip-dripping on the forehead don't hold a candle to it.

At last, she climbs down. She places the toy with due deliberation on the floor. She gives me a long, hard look. She decides I am beyond all hope. And with an expression of knowing like an old wise man, shrugs her shoulders with dramatic exaggeration, and—long blonde hair flying—exits.

I settle back on the pillow with an awful sense of having been deprived of the most rewarding five-minute slumber of the night.

Then—since I had in fact asked to be woken—Tamsin's mother plays Mutt to her Jeff (or should it be the other way round?) and yells from the kitchen: "Your porridge is getting cold!"

Well, naturally, I'm up in a trice.

Being, as I am, a great believer in warm porridge—and kindness in the morning.

1975

Help!

OK, I'm a dog person.

But it doesn't follow that I can't tell dogs from children.

For a start, there is a numerical discrepancy leg-wise. And dogs sleep more. Also dogs, when pleased, don't generally smile (some do), and pleased children scarcely ever wag their tails.

But there is one way in which dogs and children are enchantingly alike. It is in the business of being helpful.

Our dog, Muffie, is very helpful. She washes the kitchen floor with admirable thoroughness. She chases foxes out of the garden. She brings home tree trunks. The only problem is that she doesn't remember why. *Our* notion that they might be useful firewood is forgotten when she decides, once they are home, that she must have brought them here for chewing. And chewing. Finally nothing is left but chew-dust.

And there is horticulture. She knows the tools. I only have to grasp one, and she is nudging and tripping me, ready to join the dig. It's clear that it would be most unwise to take her along on an archaeological weekend. Ignoring the need for recording, dating, and cataloging, she would cause Roman shards and Stone Age flints to fly all over the site.

In our garden, I overturn a clod, and she's in there, scratching and snuffling. It's "Clear out of my way, you useless human! Digging is a dog thing. Watch and learn!" So I have to retreat and let the professional work. The fact that she tends to submerge surrounding plants with a volcanic eruption of fine soil concerns her not a whit. The hole, the *hole* is all that matters.

This is where I suspect she shares with children a basic confusion. It is the question of who, exactly, is helping whom. Is she helping me, or am I actually helping her?

When I was a very small child, my mother used to note down silly things my brother and I said or did to include them in letters to our older half-brothers away fighting for king and country. I remember her telling me about

141

one of my sayings years later.

My brother Trevor and I had evidently been playing for some time in the garden. My mother came out and asked me what I was doing.

"I'm busy helping Trevor," I squeaked.

"And what's Trevor doing?"

"He's busy helping me." That was it. Apparently, I had no more to squeak on the subject.

The classic example of children "helping" parents is washing the car.

Why do small people have this eager yen to wash the family vehicle? The answer is clear seconds after the hose has been turned on, and the suds are lathering up like a bubble bath. What began as "car cleaning" has turned spontaneously into what is known as "water play." The kids are now washing *each other*—and the cat, the shrubs, the gravel, and any passerby who foolishly fails to pass by on the other side.

The truth is that car cleaning is hard and boring, while playing with a hose is gigantic fun. I have no doubt that those who are into good parenting are indulgent on such occasions, remembering their own childhoods. One parent I know admits that there is, indeed, a fine balance to be struck when a child offers to be helpful. At the very least, children should be allowed to feel they are actually helping, even when they decidedly are not.

But there are times when this can be terribly difficult.

A friend who has lived for years in rural eastern England told me a story. One of the traditional uses of female labor in the fields was the thinning-out or "singling" of sugar beets. Beet seeds (before the development of monogerm seeds) came up in bunches. The plants had to be thinned— spaced out—leaving only the largest to grow to maturity without competition.

Because mothers couldn't just leave their youngest children at home, they would take them along; even the smallest babies in their prams. This was not popular with the babies, however. The farther the women moved along the row, the louder would grow the babies' complaining: a kind of country rhythm.

Once the children could walk, they would follow their mothers along the row. On one occasion, a mother was working away like this, with the child coming after her.

Having worked concentratedly for a time, she turned to check her child's whereabouts.

It was then, horrifyingly, that she saw stretching away behind her a long line of bare earth. Not a plant was left standing. And at the same moment she saw a small child looking very—*helpful*.

"You missed some, Mum," her young one said, "so I've pulled them up for you."

1997

You Might Have Warned Me, Miss Austen

It isn't every man who can truthfully say (and James Bond, remember, is pure fiction) that at breakfast this morning he was more or less prevented from engaging in any kind of successful nutritional dialog with his Weetabix by the over-affectionate attentions and loving embraces of a pretty little blonde girl.

Yet such was my lot. Furthermore, no sooner had I managed a certain degree of disentanglement, and therefore felt able to attempt a mouthful of egg, than the said young lady, punctuating her words with a hug that was hard to distinguish from a throttle, whispered with stage-voice intensity:

"I'm going to marry you."

I admit to being a trifle surprised at the announcement.

"Are you?" I said with unintentional quickness, lowering my egg spoon.

"YES!"—the capitalization being accompanied by an eye-to-eye gaze of exceedingly devoted rapture.

"So am I," said another voice, just behind me.

At this point, I feel that the reader may agree with me that my day had, in fact, started somewhat less than tranquilly. I needed a moment or two of calm to consider these unpredictable events. A proposal of marriage before finishing one's boiled egg is one thing, but *two* proposals!—and I still hadn't managed the slightest fragment of toast.

Such things, to be honest, can be slightly upsetting to someone who, like me, has been reared on the Victorian novel—who regards proposals of marriage to be private communications rather than public pronouncements; who believes that such proposals are invariably made by the man; that the party proposed to has some leeway in the matter; that the said proposals are best when they involve a longish period of growing intimacy; that they are generally made *after* breakfast; and—for the most part—just one at a time.

I am therefore fully aware that my sensibilities in such matters are only too easy to dismiss as mere backwardness and chauvinism. But I have nevertheless dared to describe my qualms in order to make it apparent how strangely shaken my sensibilities were.

"*But I'm already married*," I said.

In Austen, Eliot, or Hardy, these words would have been uttered in a tremulous undertone, and their effect would have been electrifying, cataclysmic. They would probably have ended Book I, and the hero or heroine at their receiving end would consequently have spent most of Book II indulging a declining and vaporous introspection.

In real life, however, there is neither decline nor fall.

Instead, this morning's imperturbable heroine said lightly, "Oh, bother!" And then, after the shortest of pauses: "Well, I'm going to marry you *again!*"

"So am I," said a voice just behind me.

Which only goes to show, I suppose, that to cope with up-to-date exigencies one simply has to develop up-to-date sensibilities.

"Come along, Melanie," said her mother suddenly, "leave Christopher alone and finish your Rice Crispies. We'll have to go in two minutes, and you haven't brushed your teeth yet."

"I want to marry him first," said Miss Melanie pettishly, and clinging to my neck, gave me another Long Look coupled with a smile of such six-year-old-temporary-toothlessness that I couldn't help reflecting that brushing them was perhaps not much more than a formality. It was certainly a useful maternal device for getting their would-be owner nearer the front door of the flat and therefore nearer her infant school.

Finally, my hostess whisked Melanie and her mischievous siblings away, and I was able to muse in a more leisurely manner on the lessons of this alarming episode.

Its dénouement was, in my opinion, something that the Victorian novelists scarcely touched upon. I can't help feeling that Miss Austen may have been a little remiss in not observing that a proposal or proposals of marriage made at breakfast, notwithstanding their importunate character, may often be effectually terminated by an imperative reference to the immediate necessity of employing a toothbrush.

1977

The Ultimate Parent?

As a non-parent, I am one of the world's great, if slightly detached, admirers of fathers, mothers, and their heroic stamina. And I believe I have now discovered—through poignant, yet admiring, exposure to it—what may be the *ultimate test* of parental dedication.

I have no idea if those manuals of parenthood one sees (and which I naturally ignore) in bookshops refer to this "ultimate test" or not, but it strikes me that intimate knowledge of nappy-technique or intricate study of weaning methods probably pale in comparison to this greatest challenge.

At this point, I feel I should perhaps point out to the sensitive reader that these are merely the observations of an outsider. They are essentially whimsical observations born of no-experience whatever except that of being a visitor, a fly-on-the-wall, in the homes of various good friends who are learning, for the first time, what being parents should, or should not, involve. They, like their children, are beginners. Everyone is a beginner at something sometime. My observations most certainly should not be taken at all seriously. They are the observations of a non-starter.

It seems to me, then, that the ability of parents—in this case one particular father—to withstand the "ultimate test" without flinching, and, better still, without losing his tolerant fondness for his offspring, surpasses in sheer intrepidity even the capacity parents possess of waking up just enough out of solid sleep in the middle of the night to perform mysterious domestic rituals relative to their offspring. This test is nobler even than their devotedly endless fetching and carrying to and from and from and to birthday parties, playschools, swimming pools, and dancing lessons—all of which their children seem to assume are part of the natural order of things—and which would frankly shudder the cockles of my self-centered and child-free heart.

This ultimate test—of which I will tell more later—was strongly (but not decisively) challenged in the fortitude league tables by an experience the father I just mentioned underwent a night or two ago. I was sound asleep

146

in the only spare bedroom. So it wasn't until breakfast that I found out what had occurred.

The father told me he had been woken, along with his wife, deep in the night, by their very small daughter. Importunately, she wanted to whisper something in her mother's more or less dormant ear. Now even I am aware that some well-regulated and more experienced parents would, at this point, have carried the child firmly back to her bed and told her to wait until breakfast. I can only think that this mother and father were too *much* asleep to think of such a disciplined approach.

It further transpired that their little girl additionally insisted that her message was completely *secret* and must be delivered *in private and only to her mother.* Her father must have been barely conscious, or I can't help feeling he wouldn't have been so easily taken for a ride. He also is a man of great modesty and ironic humor; I have no doubt that, somniferously, he found the turn of events quite funny, and looked forward to telling the tale later with all due self-deflation.

His daughter, who certainly exercises powers of persuasion out of all proportion to her size, made her two conditions quite clear. One was that her dad mustn't be anywhere near when she was telling her mother what she had to tell. The other was that there was to be no more sleep for any of them until her wish was granted.

So—criticize if you want—her father clambered mutely out of bed and swayed unseeingly out into the living room. There he collapsed with a weighty lurch into an armchair, finding himself to be starkly awake and filled with the kind of grim, determined patience that mankind experiences only at three-forty-five (or -six) in the morning.

He sat like this, waiting. He waited, and, having waited, he continued to wait. He tried hard to contrive that sort of half-stupor that makes it easier to return to instant sleep when the propitious moment comes. But the propitious moment didn't seem to come.

"Time," as Dylan Thomas wrote, "passes."

A faint glimmer of dawn glimmered faintly between the black twigs of the north London winter trees outside the window. It then began to dawn on this intrepid parent—at last—that he had been sitting in the armchair for a remarkably long stretch of the night. Suddenly, he was infused with a feeling of assertiveness.

I have, he thought (though he realized at the same moment that this was probably questionable), *RIGHTS!*

He got up—and although to say that "he marched" would not be an accurate description at all, it is nevertheless what he *intended* to do—back into the bedroom. It was then that he realized the awful truth. His daughter had gone back to bed hours ago, her probably not-very-important secret quickly imparted; his wife had been blissfully and profoundly in dreamland ever since. Both of them had forgotten to tell him that he could go back to bed....

Hearing this tale in the morning, a tale told with self-mocking and exaggerated irony, made me laugh as only the gratefully inexperienced can laugh; at the same time I felt amazed admiration for the fact that this exploited man was also chuckling delightedly at his misfortune. In short, he was telling me this story to illustrate what he felt were the wry joys of being a parent.

As he finished his story, his daughter walked into the room.

"It's time," he now qualmlessly informed her.

It was time for—well for that ultimate, make-or-break test of paternal stamina that I have already hinted at once or twice.

I should explain that this supreme-most demand of a child on fatherly duty and equanimity is not something *every* child occasions. Some children grow impressively into adulthood without it. Some impose it only haphazardly or intermittently. Some perpetrate milder versions of it that stimulate little or no angst. Others early abandon their "talent" for it, usually when they come to believe, rather sadly, that they *have* no apparent talent for it. And now and then a prodigious child, of exceptional aptitude, marvelous promise and wonderfully natural talent, appears on the scene and does nothing but amaze, please, and inspire.

But in the case of this particular father's daughter, it can't be honestly argued that she belongs to the latter category. She is willing and hopeful, without doubt, but she is not yet very *practiced*. Give her time!

It needs to be said that her father owns a grand piano and plays it well. He is an intense lover of classical music and very knowledgeable. He has a sensitive and keenly wondering ear.

He sits down at the piano.

His diminutive child takes up her correct stance.

And, as he accompanies, she applies herself with remarkable diligence and determination, if slightly less than perfect accuracy, to *her daily violin practice*.

As a mere outsider, listening, I conclude that the Yehudi Menuhin talent scouts might perhaps want her to practice a *little* longer—maybe a decade or so—before they offer her a place in his school. But her musical father is not in the least perturbed. He meticulously plays on, regardless. And he is fully awake.

1979

Snowfields

I haven't the slightest idea who owned our field.

We thought of it as "ours," even though most certainly it wasn't. Fields, however, at least in children's eyes, are not a question of ownership, but opportunity. Particularly when—one fine morning—there they are, transformed into a dazzle of snow instead of dull winter grass.

It was a long sloping field, and its lower end came to a stop by a stone wall bordering our garden. Its other, much higher end, if it didn't exactly require crampons, did make demands on short, spindly legs trying to trudge through shifty snow over bouncy grass. The last ten yards or so were much steeper than the rest and only worth the extra climbing effort (dragging the toboggan) because this sharp gradient offered the best possible start when we launched ourselves downhill into the thrilling unknown, yelling and screaming with delirious unrestraint as our increasing speed turned sliding into hurtling....

We had two methods of sledging (as we call sledding in Britain)—solo or in tandem. Our sledge (as we call a sled) was a proper, old-fashioned type, with iron runners. It was built sturdily of hardwood, meant to last—a hand-me-down from our older half-brothers. It could carry two of us, seated corrugatingly on its slats. But with both of us aboard, it had a tendency to dig into the snow rather than slip forward over it. With a lighter load of one, head first on your stomach, like a ship's figurehead, kicking off and steering with your feet out back, it usually worked far better. But most of our Yorkshire snowfalls thawed only too quickly, and sometimes we didn't even manage to achieve a packed smooth surface in time for sleek, resistless runs.

A grazing field has a variety of hazards that more purpose-built sleigh runs don't have. Sudden protuberant rocks. Large, dense tufts of grass. Mole hills. Stone walls encountered too precipitantly. Even on one occasion (though in a different field), holly bushes. This prickly species is, on the whole, best *not* rushed into, I'd say. But at least the experience gave you a firsthand idea of what Pooh must have felt when he dropped from his toy balloon into a gorse bush.

Our sledging field could, at its best, be pretty good for this winter sport. However, it's the fact of being so *very* close to the ground as you sweep over it that makes sledging something more than childish hilarity. It is after all a very close encounter with the character and undulations of the earth's surface. And in my case, it was an early inkling of what has turned into a strong and lasting affection for *fields.*

Fields, it's true, mean different things in different places. In rural England, those with most appeal have been least tampered with by heavy agricultural machinery. They have, probably centuries ago, been claimed from the wilderness, tamed, and then allowed just to function usefully. They are likely to be grazing for cattle or horses or sheep and are "cultivated" by these animals quite as much as they are cared for by the farmers.

For humans they provide exhilarating walking space—vast intakes of fresh air, a sense of proprietorial liberty. We stride over the turf—the sound earth of centuries under it, the ancient sky above—and wars and rumors of wars recede for a while. Grazing land is best. Fields full of barley or wheat can be walked *around,* and their verges are often full of natural delights, insects, and plants. But (if you want to keep the farmer sweet) you don't walk *across* these fields. The greatest pleasure in roaming over a grazed field is in a lack of constraint and prescribed direction. The only dangers are the snuffling curiosity of cows and the unwisdom of using your feet without your eyes; watching out for cow-pats (and basic quagmire, too) is a rural skill not to be pooh-poohed.

I love particularly those high, mounded fields that are like the curve of the horizon. The whole airy world is up there. You are at large. You are also magnificently alone. You are not hemmed in as you are when walking along a road. Except for sudden tractors, there is no traffic. You choose your trajectory, improvise, wander, meander, stride at will. Perhaps it is the nearest we landlubbers get to the liberating isolation so loved by and awesome to sailors.

For ten years, I lived in a farmhouse in Yorkshire, literally surrounded by such fields. There was a long rough graveled track snaking across them up to the nearest road. But that was for driving in and out. My walking ground consisted of nothing but fields. Think of it!

Fields in England, though often approximately rectangular, are far from being endlessly cloned. Seen from balloon or aircraft, their jaggy, irregular outlines are like haphazard pieces in a child's simple jigsaw puzzle. Each field has a character of its own—a fact that has brought upon them a vast array of names. Field names are, in fact, an academic study.

These are often verbal labels to make quick identification easier. But I like to think they are more than merely practical. Sometimes they still bear names of owners long since gone or crops not grown there for centuries. Shape and size and contour all come into it. John Field, an aptly named expert, has compiled more than one book on the subject. The names he lists add up to a kind of vernacular rural poetics—such as: Aspen Butts, Childs Land, Limekiln Bottom, Six Men's Mead, Plum Pudding Meadow, Worden Piddle, Yonder Piece, Zidles.... There are hundreds and thousands of them apparently.

I never knew the name of "our field." But "Zidles" would do. It means "hilly land at the side." I wonder if it is still there, waiting for snowfall and children.

2003

VIII.
Willingly to School?

Dawdling on the Way

The "day boys" were definitely different.

I suppose you could put it down to good home cooking (as opposed to the dubious school version of that art). But it was something more than cuisine. Every morning, the five of them—three were brothers—would spill self-confidently, jubilantly even, onto the school playground, as though dropping in from another world.

Nothing about their arrival recalled the "melancholy Jacques." (Remember your Shakespeare? "Then the whining schoolboy, with his satchel,/And shining morning face, creeping like snail/Unwillingly to school.")

As for the rest of us, all boarders, we didn't go willingly or unwillingly to school each day; we were already there.

I became friendly, back then, with one of the three "day boy" brothers, and sometimes I was invited to their home for a glorious Sunday afternoon. It was a giggling, riotous, exuberant, cake-and-trifle, do-what-you-like sort of time. It was everything home life should be—which is just about everything boarding-school life wasn't—however amiable this particular boarding school was.

I just heard an item on the news about the ways in which most children these days go to school in Britain—day school, I mean. Far more are delivered by car than not. This radio item was about a proposal to introduce many special high-tech school buses. Each child would swipe a card on entering the bus, and this would immediately be logged on a central computer so that parents would know their child was safely aboard. The argued advantage was that fewer cars would clog rush hour, and mothers would spend less time as taxi drivers. But there was also concern that some children who now cycle or walk to school, would be deprived of wholesome exercise and fresh air if they also resorted to a bus.

I found this enchantingly old-fashioned, I must say. To think that there may be some children—in remote country places, perhaps—who still, in our auto-dominated age, actually go by foot or pedal power to school!

If there are in fact any such energetic younglings, I don't suppose it would cut much ice with them to realize they are the tail end of a very ancient tradition. (Shakespeare's dawdling schoolboy doubtlessly dawdled on foot.)

Flora Thompson, in *Lark Rise to Candleford* (1939), describes her own late-19th century impoverished hamlet childhood. And her evocation of the children going to school suggests a continuum surely unchanged since schools first existed.

"School began at nine o'clock," she writes, "but the hamlet children set out on their mile-and-a-half walk there as soon as possible after their seven o'clock breakfast." The mothers wanted them out of the house, and the children "liked plenty of time to play on the road."

She makes you picture these shabby country boys and girls "straggled, in twos and threes and in gangs" up the long road. "In cold weather some of them carried two hot potatoes which had been in the oven, or in the ashes, all night, to warm their hands on the way and to serve as a light lunch on arrival."

On the road to and from school they were, in a way, suspended between home discipline and school discipline, and they threw off such "civilization." There was shouting, and there was quarreling ... and bullying, playing marbles, bird's nesting, snowballing, and sliding on icy puddles. *And* there was eating.

They ate turnips and pea-shanks from the fields, ears of wheat, young greens from the hawthorn hedges, sorrel leaves, blackberries, and crab apples. This was not so much because of hunger but "from habit and relish of the wild food."

Perhaps it is this age-old child culture of "going to school" that Flora Thompson was putting into words—a kind of folk memory—that objectors wish today had not been replaced by cars and buses.

For me, "going to school" was not like this. It occurred, not at the start of each school day, but at the start of each term. The schools I attended were hundreds of miles away. I traveled between home and school by train.

The first time, my parents accompanied me all the way from home in Yorkshire to Kings Cross in London. (Devotees of Harry Potter will know this major station as the place where Harry vanishes through a brick wall before embarking on the Hogwarts Express to *his* new school.)

I do not remember what happened that first time. I was told later. It seems my parents were astounded and dismayed when, met at the station by a master from the school, I just walked away with him without even saying goodbye.

In my defense, I probably had no idea what was going on. I probably misunderstood and thought I'd see them a minute or two later in another part of the station. It was not a deliberate snub, I feel certain; well—fairly certain.

After the first time, we were trusted to travel to school parentless. So *our* long road to school was this train ride, and I remember vividly that halfway-house feeling, as the train joggled and surged inevitably and relentlessly south—a feeling that was almost wild in its temporary freedom, yet at the same time full of foreboding.

Given a choice, I would have stayed at home. But I cannot deny that school life—once you were taken over by it again—involved some quite marvelous things: things that could never have happened in the home world. But first you had to cross the bridge that spanned the divide between those two largely dissimilar contexts.

The night before we had to go back to school, we always went "to the pictures." It was meant as a treat. It *was* a treat. But sitting tremulously in the dark, transported into that escapist but temporary celluloid world of Hollywood or Pinewood, was very like standing on the edge of a cliff.

You absolutely *dreaded* the doom-laden moment the credits rolled and "God Save the Queen" struck up. It meant, with the inevitability of Authoritative Decree, that this was it! THE END! The holidays were finished.

At dawn, one would have to jump off the cliff and turn back once again into a schoolboy. You'd say goodbye to the freedoms and luxuries of home for endless weeks of doing what you were told (mostly) and being subjected to Latin (too much) and longing for cakes (oh, *longing!*) and playing Rugby (badly) or cricket (worse). You'd have a cold shower every morning and eat school porridge and be known only by your last name.

As I've said, this regime had its compensations. But I've had a tingling feeling of letdown, ever since, whenever a film comes to an end.

2002

The Blue Moon Awards

The Blue Moon Awards may not have the pizazz of the Hollywood Oscars, but in and around Sunley Junior School, Glasgow, they are no small matter.

To be invested with a Blue Moon Award—they are so far confined to the ten- and eleven-year-olds in Mrs. A's Primary Six class—is not to be sneezed at.

To date, in fact, only two of the pupils, James McFadgeon and Karen McDougal, have stood at the teacher's desk for her to place the blue ribbon with its pendant blue moon around their necks, to a background of resounding applause.

Like all the best ideas, the Blue Moon Awards sort of *occurred*.

One Monday at lunchtime, Mrs. A found herself saying to a little boy with a vast capacity for naughtiness, "James McFadgeon, what on earth has happened? You've behaved properly *all morning*. Is there a blue moon in the sky?" (And she looked quizzically out of the window to check.)

The small smile on James's face hinted immense pleasure. When he went home, he even told his mother about it.

That evening, there happened to be a Parents' Night at Sunley Junior School, and James's mother went along with all the other mums and dads to chat with the teacher. When her turn came, she said, "I hear there was a blue moon in the sky today!"

And from this time forward, grew the notion of the Blue Moon Awards. On Friday, James became the very first Blue Moon Award recipient—for having behaved properly, not just for a morning or for a day but for a full five days. Something inside him had found a challenge worth striving for—a basic desire to please, perhaps, an essential preference for being good. Whatever it was, his willingness to turn over a new leaf achieved an award that carries serious value, not only for him, but for the rest of the class, too.

Immediately, Karen McDougal announced that she was going to try for a Blue Moon Award. This resolve was almost as surprising as James's. Karen, like James, was perfectly aware that she was one of the undoubted renegades in Sunley's Primary Six. This class as a whole, composed of the most unruly halves of two of last year's Primary Five classes, had exercised every ounce of Mrs. A's capacity for discipline and control.

The next week, Karen started out well. But by about Wednesday, she had slipped from grace a few times, and Mrs. A had more or less made up her mind that she could only give her a *Half* Blue Moon Award on Friday. But then something remarkable took place.

On Thursday night, Karen didn't feel at all well. First thing Friday morning, her father phoned the school. He was very puzzled. "Karen ought just to stay in bed," he said, "but she insists on getting up. She says she's been promised something at school today and *must* come into school! What on earth has she been promised?"

Karen hadn't even told her parents.

So Karen did come in, and—partly in recognition of such undoubted heroism—she was invested, as they all applauded her vigorously (and this was in spite of the fact that she had not made herself universally loved by other children in the class), with a *Full* Blue Moon Award. At lunchtime, she went home and back to bed.

Karen's Blue Moon, Mrs. A found out later, became a prominent adornment on the family Christmas tree.

And so it was that the Blue Moon Awards got started. Fourteen other children are now intent on winning one.

Actually, more of the class—all but one—wanted to try, but Mrs. A had to point out that Blue Moon Awards were really for people who had been in the habit of being bad, not for those who were generally good. And that's why Mrs. A had to introduce Gold and Silver Moon Awards as well.

1989

Such Glad Sweetness

"Slugs and snails and puppy dog's tails" were what "little boys" were "made of."

"Little girls," on the other hand—unfairly I thought—were made of "sugar and spice and all things nice."

We had a shortage of little girls at home, and later, at boarding school, a positive *dearth,* but I don't recall actually believing this sexist doggerel to be much more than a rather weird grown-up joke.

I knew, anyway, absolutely, what were *really* made of sugar and spice and all things nice, and they were infinitely more interesting than mere girls, for goodness sake. They were what Mr. Percy sold in his shop. He kept them in beautiful and delightful glass jars with enticing screw tops and delicious labels, delectably arranged in glorious lines on entrancing shelves. Their color and variety, shape and texture, hardness, softness, shine, sheen, and sugary sweetness were things of incalculable pleasure, the "stuff that dreams are made on"—sweet dreams.

In different cultures, they acquire different names—candies, sweets— and also pet names and brand names. Dylan Thomas in *A Child's Christmas in Wales* (a good read year round) lists some tongue-tingling ones from his boyhood: "Bags of moist and many colored jelly babies …. Hardboileds, toffee, fudge and allsorts, crunches, cracknels, humbugs, glaciers, marzipan, and butterwelsh for the Welsh."

Mr. Percy is the only shopkeeper I remember from my Yorkshire childhood, and I even remember exactly where his shop was on Bingley's main street. He was high on my list of puerile priorities. He must be a particularly early impression, I think, because, as I see him now, it is from a very low-lying perspective. He towers, big, round, and beamingly pink-faced, every inch a Yorkshireman, over his counter, looking down at me, his features suffused with the benevolence of marshmallow and the mouth-wateringness of peardrops, patiently awaiting my squeaked, shy order. "Could I please haf a quarterofapound of …." Mmmm, what would it be today? Paynes Poppets? Clarnico peppermint creams? Murraymints, the "too-good-to-hurry mints?" Sugared almonds?

The decision would already have been mulled over for a long while, probably with an acute sense of premature longing in bed the night before. It might be chocolate bon-bons; it might be New Berry fruits with their suddenly gushy liquid centers; it might be Sharp's toffees, buttery and chewy; it might be licorice allsorts. Should I get the toffees this week with broken nuts in them? Would I have enough pocket money left for a small bar of Cadbury's milk chocolate? Or a tube of Rolos? Spangles? Refreshers?

These were matters of grave consideration, compared to which the machinations of Hitler and the strategies of Montgomery and Eisenhower were of no significance whatsoever. In fact, I'm not entirely sure I'd even heard of Churchill, and if I had, my interest in his determination to defeat the enemy would probably have concentrated on one basic question: how soon after victory would sweet rationing end?

I suppose I ought to feel a small inkling of shame about all this. But I don't. Are today's small children any different? On the news the other morning was a brief item. The newscaster referred to a recently completed survey. Why is it that surveys, involving considerable costs and manpower, so frequently arrive at—just what we already thought we knew? This one concluded that although children "do know what's good for them, they *still* buy sweets and crisps on the way home from school."

I do not admit to falling backward in astonishment on hearing this news. I can't help wondering how the questionnaire might have been phrased.

(1) Which would you prefer to spend your pocket money on? (a) broccoli (b) rice pudding (c) Mars Bars, chocolate creams, fudge, and/or Turkish Delight.

(2) If your school lunchbox included an apple, a yogurt, and a packet of m&m's, and you were in a ship that has just hit an iceberg and is sinking fast, and the captain ordered you to throw overboard two out of the three items in your lunchbox, which item would you keep?

(3) Daily boiled cabbage or an inexhaustible supply of Rowntrees Fruit Gums. You can only have one or the other. Choose.

I feel reasonably certain of the answers.

In my own case, I continued as I had begun. When I went away to school, the extraordinary lure and appeal of the sweet was, if anything, intensified. At the beginning of each school term, my mother put together an incomparable "tuck-box" filled with fierce and poignant reminders of home: lemon cake, sponge cake, chocolate cake, marmalade cake, jam tarts, mince pies, rock buns, tangerines, nuts, and all kinds of chocolates and sweets. What a contradiction in terms all this generosity was! She packed us off to life in a distant and Spartan school, my brother and me, with every imaginable goody—the very treats that were NOT featured in school meals. Looking back now, I suspect that she may not have much liked the thought of us going away to school, but it was "the thing to do." She confessed much later to me that she had loathed school herself. So I think the "tuck" was an attempt to soften the blow, and—for the very few weeks it lasted—it did just that.

I remember, at my first school, we were eventually allowed to walk to the nearest shop—a mile there and back—once we were "seniors." This was just once a week. And we could buy sweets. It was a privilege I rated rather close to a state of paradise.

At the school we went to when we were older, my first and last attempt at becoming a manufacturing businessman occurred. A few of us started making batches of fudge to sell to other boys. We were somewhat successful and even made enough money once to afford a midnight feast of almost Roman luxury at the end of the term.

But the enterprise was a bit hazardous, and I have not attempted homemade candy since. Two untowardnesses were involved. The first was Vesuvial. Something in our method of cooking the fudge was chemically uncertain. After we smoothed it into the trays, expecting to cut it into bite-sized rectangles once it cooled, the mixture would sometimes, with no warning, start to fizz, spit, and erupt like a volcano. It was alarming, hilarious, and financially unviable.

The other hazard, I confess, was more predictable, if almost as uncontrollable.

We ate almost as much as we sold.
2002

The Taylor

The intonation of his voice—a deliberating, mellifluous murmuration—was an irresistible gift to schoolboy mimics.

Hardly the first schoolmaster in history (or in our school) to invite such adulation, Mr. Taylor was unusual in his disarming habit of mimicking us mimicking him. Finally, it became impossible to tell who had started the game. Were we teasing him or he us?

Teacher of sixth-form English literature and director of school plays, "The Taylor" (did we really call him this behind his back, or am I inventing?) knew, of course, that imitation can sometimes be high flattery. He also knew that it is often an excellent way of memorizing things. So he would come into his classroom intoning by means of a long purr of feline syllabics some quotation he particularly wanted us never to forget. And he would punctuate this with a unique up-down waggle of his index finger. Naturally, we also repeatedly imitated this idiosyncrasy. And like parrots, we memorized his words. We didn't forget them.

To this day, I can, and do, quote snatches and tatters of Chaucer, Shakespeare, Donne, Pope, Milton, Keats, Byron, Coleridge, Wordsworth, Hopkins, Eliot, and others that The Taylor bequeathed to us in imitable utterance.

His bequest was sometimes rather more than a snatch or two. Eliot's "The Love Song of J. Alfred Prufrock" was a Taylor favorite, and I can't possibly be the *only* survivor from that class who still periodically announces: "I am measuring out my life with coffee spoons," or murmurs *sotto voce:* "I grow old … I grow old …/I shall wear the bottoms of my trousers rolled," or observes, when the mood strikes, that "In the room the women come and go/ Talking of Michelangelo." Longer stretches of the poem remain with me, too, rolling around in my head and sallying forth into the unwitting airwaves at inappropriate intervals.

I must say, though, that anyone overhearing me must wonder why such memorable words emerge in a voice quite unlike my own, the vowels elasticated Taylor-fashion: "Ta-a-a-l- k iiiiinggggg o-o-o-f Miiiiii chel a-a-a-a-a-ng-ell ooohhhh!"

To non-cognoscenti, I admit, it must seem novel, to say the least. But would they think it more natural if I were to imitate Eliot's own weirdly desiccated rendering of his poetry? If Mr. Taylor (and I have no idea what his first name was) conveyed one thing above all to us—even if it was by means of genial eccentricity—it was an appreciation of the fascinating *sound* of words. A sound not just as an adjunct to meaning, but essentially suffused into meaning.

"With beaded bubbles winking at the brim" (Keats) and "Busy old fool, unruly sun" (Donne) are indelibly Taylor-voiced for me. In my year, he taught no Tennyson. I'm not sure he even liked that Victorian eminence. But why do I vividly remember "Break, break, break,/On thy cold gray stones, O Sea!/And I would that my tongue could utter/The thoughts that arise in me," with such a measured musical insistence? If I didn't first hear these honeyed words quoted by The Taylor, why is it I now hear them in his voice?

Mr. Taylor was a musician, as well. This was an Anglican school, and he played the chapel organ. There he was, ensconced in elevated remoteness up in the organ loft, like a soul in glory—or at least in possession of a love of thundering, trumpeting, raging, booming, cacophonous, rip-roaring demonstrativeness and energy that made it hard to distinguish the man from the instrument, sounding out their vast and manifest destiny in that resonant architectural setting.

In some ways, his "organist's hat" was in contrast to others The Taylor wore. In play rehearsals, or in his class, he never roared. He had no discipline problems. But this control was achieved by *character,* by warm-hearted irony, and by that almost inexplicable capacity only the truest teachers possess to convey the idea that their subject is an indispensable part of life, yet at the same time something quite casual and lighthearted.

Only on the rarest occasions did I see him work himself up to give us a downright telling off—and it was an impressively unconvincing performance. Even he didn't seem to see the point of it. He might make the organ rage or show us how to *act* fury, rousing us, for instance, to elocute Lear's impotent, anguished "Blow, winds, and crack your cheeks! Rage, blow! You cataracts and hurricanoes, spout … " and so on and so forth, but he was himself *far* too tolerant of human nature, amused by its silly foibles, and too disengaged from such absurdities as boys behaving badly to be *genuinely* angry.

If I had seriously wanted to be a schoolteacher, my preferred model would have been The Taylor.

But then that would have required some kind of *genius*.

1998

The Herrick Event

What is that tune? I am humming it to myself with all the absent-mindedness of Winnie the Pooh. I catch myself doing it, in fact.

"Pom-p-pom-pom pom PAAAAM POM!" A neat change of key on that last note—or at least, since I am not much above the humming, brainless bear in musical know-how, it is what I *take* to be a key change. But ignorance of bee behavior was no deterrent to The Bear's enjoyment of honey, so, regardless of my uncertain musicianship, I hum on unabashed: "Pa-paaa p-pa pa paaa pa PAR!" And then I have the gall to move enthusiastically into the refrain....

But what *is* this tune?

My goodness! In all its awfulness, it suddenly comes flooding back. As the boy-narrator observes in Alexander Cordell's *Rape of the Fair Country*: "It is strange that memory will fade on some things and hang like hooks on to others." Strange indeed. The awesome memory of the experience connected with this tune should probably have been "unhooked" long ago. And yet, I don't know. Perhaps it was one of those salutary experiences that keep you ever so 'umble and so can't be entirely bad.

Herrick!—yes, Robert Herrick, that's the man! Not the American author of *The Common Lot.* No. My Robert Herrick was an English country parson of the time of Charles I. He was a Caroline poet with a delight in rustic myths, fancies, and ballads. He's the one all right. And frankly, I have a bone to pick with him.

Yes, indeed, Mr. Herrick, it is you I hold responsible for one of the most embarrassing ten minutes of my entire life—no, no, *the* most embarrassing. Even the time I strongly advised a woman in a New York bookstore not to order a dozen copies of a certain book—even that was fractionally less frightful. "Why not?" she asked.

"Unreadable," I replied.

"How very interesting," she said. "I'm the author."

The Herrick Event took place at my boarding, or "public," school, as we enigmatically call these actually *private* schools in Britain. The new headmaster, impeccably qualified for the job because of his muscular devotion to both Rugby Football and Hymn Practice, instituted a new "House Competition."

It was a *singing* competition—part-singing. Now you'd think that the powers-that-were, having searched my records for any indication of a musical propensity and having found none, would have hastily withdrawn my name from the list of potential participants. But it seems that 1957 was a bad year, in our house, for tenors. There really is no other explanation for my press-ganging, though the inexperience of the teacher given the task of training us four may also have had a bearing.

The piece we were to sing began: "Gather ye rose-buds while ye may,/Old Time is still a-flying:/And this same flower that smiles to-day/To-morrow will be dying."

That was it, and more of the same—four verses in all. Mr. Herrick wrote the words sometime back in the 17th century. He had *no idea* what he was letting me in for.

This song was a very peculiar choice, now I come to consider the matter, for 16- and 17-year-old boys to sing—and in front of the whole school as well. Somehow I never got to see the poem's title (I was probably too distracted by trying to grasp the apparently important difference between crotchets and semi quavers, or quarter notes and sixteenth notes), but turning it up now in my *Oxford Book of English Verse,* I find it is called "To the Virgins, to Make Much of Time."

Yes, that's right—I did say Herrick was a parson.

We practiced. And we practiced. The tenor part was given particular attention. It needed it. "Ga - ther ye rose buds while yeee m a y/Old Time is still a- fly- yi- y i n g."

I hadn't a clue.

The dreaded night came. I still hadn't a clue. Our house was on third. The first "team" produced a mellifluous glee performed with exquisite delicacy and fastidious timing. The second was even better: crisp articulation, extravagantly complex fa-la-falala's, an intricate warp-and-weft of song to make you gasp. Headed for an engagement at the Albert Hall they were and smug of face to boot.

And then it was our turn. The very words of our song, of course, simply *invited* that initial titter among the youngest boys in the front row. Astoundingly, though, the first line seemed to go all right, and the next line almost gave one a sense of confidence. *Perhaps I'm better at this than I thought,* I thought. A moment of ambition there: all those years of clandestine singing in the bath had borne fruit after all....

Looking back on it (which I still can't do with total equanimity), I suspect that it was the sin of ambition that undid me. That and the Gap. The Gap was a trial to me. The tenor part stops at one point while the three others continue upping-and-downing variously. The tenor (not much of a mathematician at the best of times) counts in silence. And then he joins in again. This is the Gap.

The Gap arrived. I fell silent. I counted. And I joined in again. The result was an instant cacophony terrible for the listeners and excruciating for the singers. The front-row titters spread like unruly ripples in a pond, soon reaching the fourth-form thugs halfway back. Even the prefects at the very back were beginning to raise amused eyebrows.

I stopped. I must have been too soon. So I counted a bit more. And then I blurted into song again—oh! Oh! OH!—worse. *Far* worse. I took a deep breath then, a long, deep breath. The others were still going manfully—you would have been proud of them, Mr. Herrick. But for me the room was now whirling. Mayhem was breaking out with increasing volume and fiendish delight in the audience. Titters had grown to universal chuckling. Once more, I thought (now reduced to nothing but bravery and pinkness) once more into the breach, dear—wait for it—should I? Shouldn't I?—NOW!

"And this same flower that ...."

It was like—like nothing on earth. The words, for harmony's sake, withered on my lips, once and for all. Finally. My career was over. I would never sing in public again. Possibly not even in private. The remaining trio kept on as well as they could, mercifully, but rather forlornly tenor-less. After a very long, long time they reached:

"For having lost but once your prime,/You may forever ta-a-arry."

It was over. The applause was *tremendous.* Uproarious. We slunk ignominiously off the platform.

The fourth and last House Team came up in our place and sang, with unsurpassable musicianship, John Ward's "Retire, My Troubled Soul." Its Jacobean melancholy seemed to me a bitter truth:

"Retire, my troubled soul,/Rest, and behold thy days of dolour, dangers manifold./See, life is but a dream, whose best contenting,/Begun with hope, pursued with doubt, enjoyed with fear,/Ends in repenting."

Yea, verily.

But today, as I'm humming and remembering, I'm with the laughers, really—and I can comfort myself retrospectively with a little more knowledge of Herrick. Apart from writing some enchanting poetry (remember "Whenas in silks my Julia goes/Then, then, methinks, how sweetly flows/The liquefaction of her clothes"?), he also seems to have been endowed with a good sense of humor. So he probably would have enjoyed our performance.

After all, it is a marvelous sonnet of his that is called "Delight in Disorder." There is encouragement, methinks, in that. And I do hum him still. In secret.

1985

IX.
Flower and Veg

Asparagus and Other Flights of Fancy

A man may have ambitions over the age of 27, whatever they say.

Two spring to my mind. One is to go up in (or just under) a balloon. This is my airy ambition.

My earthy ambition is to grow asparagus.

Not just grow it, but grow it with such aplomb that I could go out to the asparagus bed of an April/May morning and slice off a sufficient number of perfect, tender, succulent four-inch buds to make a meal. Or a first course, anyway. What more could a gardener ask for?

Yet the amateur horticultural world is littered with resignedly shoulder-shrugging would-have-been asparagus-growers, including moi.

"Have you ever tried growing asparagus?" is a good question to toss at over-confident gardeners.

"Oh, I tried once," they mutter.

And then unaccountably the conversation switches to their prize-winning *leeks*.

Even Alfred W. Kidner, author of the only book I've found devoted to asparagus, notes "the apparent indifference of asparagus to all attentions of man."

And A. A. Milne, in a classic essay on asparagus, has these only-too-accurate words to say: "Theoretically, an asparagus bed takes three years to mature. Practically what happens is that after the second lean year you decide, very naturally, to grow carrots instead. ... [After] two years of carrots you decide, again very naturally, to give asparagus one more chance, and after ... another two barren years you decide ... on spinach. ... So in a little while you will have been trying to grow asparagus for eight years, and you will have come to the conclusion (as I have) that the thing cannot be done. You can buy asparagus, you can eat asparagus (heavens, yes), but you can't grow it. ... "

Like Mr. Milne, I have tried.

Following advice, I dug down virtually to Australasia (I lived in Yorkshire

173

then) and compiled a bed for the spider-rooted specimens that was layered, like a marvelous chocolate cake, with loam and manure. I planted the plants. Nothing happened, except for one wispy finger meandering above the surface. It stretched plaintively skyward, turned into a windblown feathery fern, died down in the autumn, and then vanished forever.

I am, however, now determined to try again. Partly this is prompted by childhood memories of the asparagus beds in my grandmother's garden in Norfolk. They were the only successful asparagus beds I've known. They convince me—despite Milne—that the vegetable *can* be grown.

With her terrier, Sprigginsgrass, in the bicycle basket, my aunt, who lived with Granny, used to trail me alongto feed the horse and the hens, collect the eggs—and pick the asparagus. It grew in two specially mounded squares of dark, weedless earth with scrupulously sloped boundaries. This asparagus corner was surrounded by beech hedges. The asparagus was invisibly subterranean except for the new shoots, thick thumbs, and slender fingers emerging haphazardly like a conjuring trick. A similiar trick is performed by mushrooms: they seem to come from nowhere, like dew or manna.

Auntie Jo cut the ones she judged ready with matter-of-fact pride. We took the purplish-green and white spears across the road to the house, handing them in at the kitchen. Twenty minutes later, we were dipping them into melted butter at the dining-room table, gorging the delicacy like kings.

Milne describes this pleasure wonderfully (though he advocates Hollandaise sauce). "Real asparagus," he writes, "must be eaten to the hilt, so that the last bite imperils the thumb." And he observes how "tender fragments … will crumble off from each shoot as you have it in the sauce, and be left, green islets in a golden sea, marooned upon the plate." Then he adds, "These must be secured at any cost with the fingers, a spoon, a piece of bread, an old envelope, it matters not. When you are eating asparagus, you are eating asparagus. Reserve your breeding for the brussels sprouts."

The thing, of course, that above all drives me to have another go at asparagus culture is the thought of eating it (the asparagus, I mean, not the culture). You can buy professional bunches of it easily enough, but these are almost flavorless. They don't hold a candle to the taste I remember from years ago. But another thing drives me, too—a great unwillingness to admit defeat.

There isn't a gardening book on my shelves that does not try to persuade me that there is nothing more to asparagus growing than planting, feeding, weeding, and waiting. Any fool can do it, the experts suggest. Even Mr. Kidner, who states that it is easier to design and make a car than to grow asparagus well, remarks: "If thistles grow well [in your soil], so will asparagus. The same applies to couch grass." Since these two rank weeds will grow well on any soil (they colonize my plot at the drop of a hat), Kidner's remark is more infuriating than enlightening.

Anyway, this time I am attacking the problem from several different directions at once. I have bought plants, grown in pots, from a garden center. A mail order of crowns will come from an asparagus grower who happens to have a nursery in Loddon, the village my grandmother lived in. And Monty, a lady who has one of the local allotments, has sown a packet of seed for me. She swears by this method. All these are a great incentive to longevity and continuing aspirations—which brings me back to balloons.

My wife's Christmas present to me was a voucher for a balloon ride. Riding in a balloon is almost as unpredictable, though, as the growing of asparagus; it is so weather-dependent. You book a date and time. Phone on the day. You are told your the flight is cancelled. You book another day. And so it goes. The question is, which is going to happen first? Will I still be waiting patiently for my ballooning eight years later, as Milne had to for his asparagus?

A happy thought strikes me, though: maybe the two ambitions will finally *coincide*. The Reverend Sidney Smith claimed that heaven was eating paté de foie gras to the sound of trumpets. I don't hold with that at all! Heaven is *eating homegrown asparagus high up in a balloon basket.* I'll let you know how things turn out.

1998

The Meaning of Gardens

What on earth is it about gardens, I occasionally ask myself, (well, about once every ten years) that seizes me?

Is it my Englishness that renders me prone? It does seem that a disproportionate number of my fellow countrymen are similarly obsessed or possessed or whatever it is.

I remember a painter saying that he thought the reason there were so few British art collectors was because they were all out in their gardens. It would seem that gardens do for us what art does for others. Certainly the dedication and daring of great British *plant* collectors of the past is no less wildly self-sacrificing than the bloodhound instincts of great *un*-British art collectors. Who could decide which is more devoted to pure pursuit—a plant hunter like George Forrest or an art hunter like Peggy Guggenheim?

Yet it's not true to say that there are no great British art addicts or, conversely, that *all* British people are gardeners. I know fine persons on this island, epitomizing all that's best in our national character, who nevertheless can't (or worse, don't want to) distinguish a buttercup from a butterfly, not to mention a pansy from a poppy.

So, as an explanation of why I am such a hortiphile, mere British blood is not enough.

Nor is it enough to put it down just to a "collector's instinct" (though collecting can often be a vigorous incentive in a gardener). Apart from bottles and parking tickets, I can't say I am myself overwhelmingly a collector. A *real* collector is without doubt surrounded from birth by an ever-increasing environment of everything he lays his hands on. In fact, a collector lays his hands on whatever is near and then doesn't take them off it again. He starts to classify and count and grade—and soon he has an overriding desire not only to bring into his kingdom all species of one genus but all species of all genera.

Perhaps the explanation of my gardening zeal is that I visualize myself as a tamer of the wild. Like Cyrus (according to Sir Thomas Browne), could it be that I am pursuing the "dictate of my education" by bringing "the treasures of the field into rule and circumspection?" The idea appeals up to a point, I admit.

But one thing is absolutely certain: I am *not* a retired army officer.

In Ronald Blythe's classic *Akenfield*, an anatomy of people living in the eastern English county of Suffolk, one of his interviewees had this to say: "About seventy percent of the gardens open to the public in East Anglia belong to ex-military men. I think it must be something to do with time and order. They love complete order and nobody can stop them imposing it on a garden.... You see, gardening allows them to go on having routine, order, tidiness, straight edges, upright posts. You can be strict in a garden."

Well, yes, but a visitor to *my* small effort at a garden might just possibly observe that in its current state of development, it is stylistically at odds with itself. The strict-and-formal rubs shoulders with the meandering-and-informal, even if they are strange bedfellows.

In part, my garden shows a marked appreciation for—though hardly a likeness to—the best of the "picturesque" tradition. Here is planting run rampant. It's a tribute to the designer William Robinson and his easy naturalness—plants amassed, chaotic, vying for place and attention—a hotchpotch. It is the kind of abandon and freedom that I hope celebrates the opulent way plants grow and flower in nature.

But then other aspects of this half-formed garden indicate a (very amateur) admiration for the parterres and knots and intricate geometries of formal, classical garden design. I am overstating the case immoderately, of course; it would take a remarkably perceptive eye to see in my unfinished patch what, after all, remains largely a figment of my imagination.

Imagination.... Now, maybe that's it. I think I may have hit on the crux of the matter.

It isn't just Englishness or acquisitiveness or even the fascination of taming the wild. Nor is it, in fact, several other attractions to the process of gardening, such as a feel for the earth, pride of ownership, or economics—all of which are admittedly factors in my complete affection for the art. No, "imagination" somehow seems to come much closer. What gardening *engages,* above all, is the imagination.

But to say that imagination is at the back of a fascination for gardens and gardening, is not necessarily to say that this fascination is therefore inevitably to do with such things as the "mystery" or "magic" of secret gardens. The notion of a garden as a place of seclusion, enclosure, privacy, or self-contained pleasure is a given. But T. S. Eliot seems to me to suggest in "Burnt Norton" that the dream of a primal, enclosed garden might not be everything its apparent innocence might suggest:

> Footfalls echo in the memory
> Down the passage which we did not take
> Towards the door we never opened
> Into the rose-garden. My words echo
> Thus, in your mind ....

> .... Other echoes
> Inhabit the garden. Shall we follow?
> Quick, said the bird, find them, find them,
> Round the corner. Through the first gate,
> Into our first world, shall we follow
> The deception of the thrush? Into our first world....

Eliot's thrush is a deceiver. Eden, Paradise, the medieval virgin's walled garden—these are, topographically, mere idealistic and mythical fantasies rather than places you might imagine as real. Images of them seem to me, for all their enchantment, always to beg the question: "So what is *outside* such carefully tended sanctuaries?"

Nevertheless, the concept of the "secret," walled garden does, in certain respects, come close in feeling to a sort of quintessence. Such a garden is so much more special than other *places*. I have felt this more richly than anywhere else, perhaps, at Sissinghurst, the famous garden of Vita Sackville-West and Harold Nicolson.

With marvelous good fortune, I first saw this garden after hours; two of us were generously allowed to have a place to ourselves that is usually swarming with visitors.

It was then that I encountered the walled "cottage garden." It was turning to dusk as we explored it, and it just happened to be suffused with precisely the right kind of softly intense light—for this, as an admirer wrote, "is an evening garden, all deep orange, yellow, gold, warm reds. I saw it first in the evening, and it was like a close, magical, fire-glowing room: she [Vita Sackville-West] called it 'the sunset garden.' It is a neat confusion—red and orange geums and wallflowers, pale gold iris, deep, dark brooms, peach-colored mimulus; everywhere old gold and copper, bronze and crimson."

You might call it "magical." But not supernatural. I can't begin to subscribe to the notion of Findhorn fairies. Such "magic" and "mystery" seem to carry one too easily into a realm of midsummer madness. I don't *talk* to flowers.

So ...?

In the end, perhaps I can only say for certain what it isn't, rather than what it is, that gardens stir in me. But I think I know my place, my clearly defined role, in relation to a garden. It is a work of art, but it isn't man*made*, precisely. The artist-gardener can't really fool himself into thinking, "I made this." Far too many surprises and seasonal changes are involved. Unexpected wonders are the lifeblood of this art, well outside the artist's control—except insofar as he can intend, and hope, and *imagine*.

Imagination is definitely integral to it: there is burning incentive in the vivid imaging of seed-become-brilliance or root-become-stem or parts-become-whole—in the realization of disparateness cohering and cooperating to define a place.

In the eye of the mind, here is a place I can include. I contain it. In this way, some of its transience can be grasped and held, and some of its permanence, continually altering, can never be stale.

1976

Summer Can Start Now

Round here, there are two infallible signs of summer. They are inextricably interwined.

The first is Maureen.

The second is a small, airy wildflower with smooth-edged, narrow leaves, filamental stems and—perched delicately at the ends of these stems—a dancing array of minuscule white daisy-like blooms with radiating petals. A tiny constellation.

Maureen is the lady who dog-sits next door. She's done it for several years now. She reappears every time the owners go on vacation or are living it up at their other house in Spain.

When Maureen climbs up the hill from the bus stop and crunches through the front gate, Thumper and Daisy are suddenly in a state of optimal, brimming, wide-eyed ecstasy. They stage a welcome jubilant enough to destabilize the equilibrium of this quiet neighborhood for a day or two. I suspect they like her even better than their real owners. After all, Maureen (who answered the ad for a dog-sitter because, she told me, "I was really *missing* having dogs around me") gives them wall-to-wall, dawn-to-dusk, 101 percent attention.

She treats them, in fact, to a ceaseless round of entertainment, most importantly throwing tennis balls and engaging in enthusiastic ramblings along the wild, natural area that slopes below our houses down to the bank bordering the motorway.

It's amazing how frequently either my wife or I, when we are taking our dogs out, bump into Maureen down there on her first, second, or third walk of the day. It is a place of liberty for dogs to run safely in. They leap and dart in this ocean of summer grasses and reeds, plunge through the white lace of the cow parsley, and weave through the yellow buttercups. The buttercups! This year they need to be seen to be believed. Talk about multiplication. It is a cosmos of pointillist yellow dots. Trillions of small suns.

I heard an astronomer on the radio the other day being asked if he could convey, without resort to the usual ungraspable figures, the quantity of stars in the sky. "What," he replied, "if we were to say there are about the same number of stars as there are blades of grass in the world?"

If he had said, "As many stars as there are buttercup heads just now in the wild area on Glasgow's southside where Maureen and other locals exercise their dogs," I would still have been dumfounded. But blades of grass! I can't even try to begin to have a go at attempting to make a stab at grasping such numbers. All I know is that the grass in this wild place is magnificently various, splendidly rampant, and, not being mowed to make hay or shorn lawns, it goes through all the stages of maturing. It shoots, flowers, and seeds without interference, like an old-fashioned meadow allowed just to do its own thing under the sky.

All this summertime growing and burgeoning enormously appeals to Maureen, nature lover extraordinaire. I know because she keeps saying so. "Do you realize how fortunate you are to live near this?" And she gazes across the waves of yellow and green, rippling and swaying in the wayward Scottish breeze, with a rapt look on her face.

One day, I was greeted by Maureen and her sister Betty up near home. "Have you seen the amazing flower that grows by the gate in the fence down by the motorway?" she asked. "I've never seen it in my life. Have a look next time you're down there. Perhaps you'll know its name. It's a lovely wee thing."

Next time I was down there, I hunted for this astonishing plant, wondering how I had failed to see it before. The footpath runs parallel to the fence. The gate is about halfway along. I looked. And I looked again, … and then I saw it. This was the kind of modest and fragile summer wildflower that cyclists and joggers and time-watching dog-walkers—anyone with his head in the air and looking forward rather than focusing on the ground at their feet and concentratedly searching for nature's minutiae-world—could easily overlook.

I had no notion of its name.

I tweaked off a fragment of stem and flower, and when I got home again, out came the books. It took some finding, but in the end, I felt sure I'd identified it. So I tore off a strip of white typing paper and inscribed its name in large silver letters on it. I then went next door and pushed it through the front door letterbox.

It was a day or two before I saw Maureen once more, and I was surprised she didn't immediately mention the name of the plant. After some chat, I eventually said, "So now you know what the plant is called."

"What plant?"

"The little white one by the gate you liked so much."

"How would I know what it's called?"

"I put it through the front door."

"You did?" Pause. "I never saw it. I must have scooped it up with the rest of the mail. I'll go and look."

She found it in the end. And now, every year, Maureen and Betty and I all watch out to see if this delightful plant is thriving and spreading. We weren't sure at first this year. But it has, it turns out, shifted position a little along the grass verge, that's all. We think there is more of it than last year, and now, a couple of weeks after Maureen started once again to act *in loco parentis*, it is fully out and sparkling away with as much verve as ever.

And that is how it has come about that Maureen and a plant that goes under the odd name of "Lesser Stitchwort"—though I am thinking of renaming it Maureen's Flower—and the arrival of summer, are all part and parcel of each year's cycle.

If the weltering buttercups are a macrocosm of vivid little suns, Maureen's flower is a microcosm of minute stars. I wouldn't be without either. And neither, I suspect, would Maureen.

2003

Gifts ... and Gifts

I'm not talking to Jimmy Hughes. He's pulled his first turnips. How dare he! Mine are a mere hand-span high, their roots so far mean and thready. Jimmy's are mature and magnificent, their 18-inch leaves a fanfare of green with their roots plump white globes.

"How do you do it?" I asked. He smiled smugly, imparting no secrets. Then, to add insult to injury, he gave me a fistful of them!

Actually, I thanked Jimmy sincerely. I even promised I wouldn't pretend, when I got them home, that I'd grown them. But officially I am still not talking to him.

We plotters are a touch competitive, but it's nothing serious. A gift of produce may be a disarming way of saying, "Look how good my crop is," but it is still, after all, a gift.

From the moment I first had a plot, I was aware of the undoubted pleasure plotters take in giving other plotters plants or vegetables. More than once I arrived at my plot, still then a passable replica of a primeval wilderness, to find a bag of potatoes, a head of lettuce, some spinach, a bunch of parsley, or leek plants hanging on the fence or deposited near the gate. I was more than touched by this generosity. It was like a welcome, an acceptance.

These gifts were usually anonymous. Part of the game is that you then have to find who grew them—the Macleods, Red, Big Ted, Joe Gallagher....

Monty was the first. Her presents tended to be of more permanent things: raspberry canes, comfrey (for its virtues as a composting plant), and a handful of knobby Jerusalem artichoke roots. I took them home, and we ate them. I told her how good they were. "You were meant to *plant* them!" she exclaimed. "Not *eat* them." She gave me some more.

I do like Jerusalem artichokes to eat, but growing them has its hazards. They spread like wildfire. They grow to ten ungainly feet and fall and break too easily in Glasgow winds. This is not comfortable for nearby vegetables. Also—and Monty did warn me—if you want to move or eliminate them, they do not make it easy. The least rootlet left in the earth sprouts with every

intention of reaching its full height again by next October. There are gifts ...
and gifts.

When I look around my plot, the plants I most appreciate are the ones that
arrived as gifts. Red chard coming up nicely from seed sent me by the visiting
artist who comes over now and then from the other side of Scotland, to sketch
in the allotments. She also gave me my three stupendous globe artichokes—
or are they cardoons? Nobody seems too sure.

Collards almost visibly bigger by the day are from a splendid parcel of
seeds mailed as a surprise by an American friend. Marigolds from Jeannie's
seed (because I admired them). Red's rhubarb. Half a dozen "perpetual"
spinach plants Tommy Docherty proffered the day before yesterday. And
Bob O'Neill's borage. Bob (although everyone else, for some reason, calls
him Robert) has been promising me some of his borage for ages, and now he's
appeared with two fine plants. I hadn't the heart to tell him I had finally sown
my own a month ago. In no time now, I'll have plenty to give away myself.

Allotment giving (and naturally I do my best to reciprocate) is an
extension of something that occurs among gardeners in general. It is a happy
survival of primitive bartering, or just the generous sharing of superfluity in
a world where virtually everything is price tagged.

Tonight we ate Jimmy's turnips. They tasted wonderfully fresh. And
better still, they tasted free. Oh, I don't know. Maybe I'll start speaking to him
again.

*(From "The Plot so Far," a weekly series about a municipal garden or
"allotment" in Glasgow, Scotland)*

1999

On Not Giving Up Supermarkets Just Yet

"Let me put it this way," observed Neil, surveying my plot early in the season. His face wore a rather mischievous look. At that time, my rows of newborn seedlings represented promise rather than fulfillment. Other than premature rhubarb, there was nothing actually edible in sight.

"Let me put it this way." (Neil likes to repeat himself.) "It looks great. But don't give up Safeway Supermarkets just yet."

"Don't worry!" I laughed with all due self-deprecation. But I did think it was a bit cheeky. After all, *his* plot last year was 90 percent covered in carpets (and you can't eat those). While this proved to be a major weed deterrent, it was also somewhat anti-veggie.

Apart from a narrow row of Jerusalem artichokes and, clambering up his boundary fence, a line of sweetly flowering sweet peas (and you can't eat those either), the nearest thing to fresh vegetables on Neil's territory in 1998 were his *plastic bags*. He had filled these with heavy dirt and dotted them around to hold down his carpeting against west winds.

I observed these bags quizzically; what struck me with the force of irony was the supermarket slogan printed on them: "Sainsbury's: Where Fresh Food Costs Less." *So that*, I thought, *is where Neil gets his vegetables*. (I knew he didn't grow them.)

The thing is, though, that the places where fresh food really "costs less" are plots like ours—well, the really successful ones, that is: carefully cultivated, personally grown vegetable patches. Supermarket vegetables are admirably standardized and washed and waxed and weighed almost to extinction, but dew fresh and better tasting they are not. One wouldn't mind these big-chain boys making persuasive claims—Sainsbury's latest is "Making Life Taste Better"—if they didn't, in the process, bag what should be *our* slogans. We are the ones making life taste better.

Weirdly, there is something about community gardens (we call them allotments in Britain) that acts as a fatal attraction to those who make money developing land for the ever increasing number of supermarkets that open each year up and down this small country. Allotments seem *peculiarly* attractive, being seen by such characters as mere wasteland, and often conveniently inner-urban to boot. And what could possibly be more *rational* and *sensible* than to take over ground where local people have for decades grown local produce for themselves, their families, and friends; to deprive them of this opportunity, and then to sell to these same local people tomatoes grown in Israel and salads flown from Africa?

Now and then, the plans of these crass developers fail, and the allotment-holders win against them. And I have to admit that I do *not* restrain my jubilation whenever this occurs.

Of course, to be realistic, we don't all manage to feed ourselves exclusively with what we grow. I have, myself, never really dreamed of what sanguine friends-of-the-soil dubbed complete "self-sufficiency." Nor do I have ambitions for my plot to be exotic—the sort of place where "[t]he nectarine, and curious peach,/Into my hands themselves do reach," in Andrew Marvell's succulent 17th-century words. His poem "The Garden" was definitely not about a breezy and rather wet Glasgow plot. No—I'm happy to leave the peaches and nectarines (and the melons and peppers) to warm-climate specialists and cognoscenti. Let them supply such juicy, heat-loving luxuries to the supermarkets, along with the oranges and lemons. As for me, I'll stick to broccoli and beans, the beets and the peas, the zucchini and the sprouts; these beat the supermarket's offerings hands down.

Now it's August. We are entering into the fruits of our labors. Even Neil's carpets (he is known around the allotment as "The Carpet Man") have parted like the Red Sea allowing a few vegetables to flourish. And his 1999 sweet peas are an admirable and wondrous curtain of color. He is picking bunches to give to his girlfriends. You simply can't buy bunches of fresh sweet peas, which have a scent like nectar and the hues of rainbows, in supermarkets.

It has been rather warm for Scotland this summer. Most years our harvesting is a steady affair, a little to pick or dig each day. This year, though, I find there is a degree of rush. My short row of peas, for example, raced through the usually more leisurely stages of unready, almost ready, ready, and finished within the space of about four days. If I really *wanted* this kind of hectic schedule, I'd move back to New England!

But here, even in old Scotland, I have been arriving home from the plot with far too much of everything far too soon—bulging bags of peas and turnips, spinach and raspberries—we have raspberry jam coming out of our ears—broad beans, and even, a first for me on this patch, some carrots.

Heavy, bulging bags on every kitchen surface! And, in spite of them being filled with my own plot-grown produce, printed on these bags are the words "Safeway: Lightening the Load." Life is full of such delicate ironies. I mean, I can't possibly give up supermarkets. If I did, where would I get all my *good, fresh plastic bags from?*

(From "The Plot so Far," a weekly series about a municipal garden or "allotment" in Glasgow, Scotland)
1999

X.
Protestations

Lord Northcliffe and the Thin Fireman

Dylan, for all we know, may just have taken a sudden liking to the smallest room in the house. He is, after all, very much the smallest member of the Welch family; his age is still counted in months rather than years.

Anyway, Dylan, whatever the reason, went and got himself stuck in there. Locked in. Unable to get out. Dylan's mum wanted to get him out, of course, but found she couldn't. All the same, she was not worried. She's not the worrying kind.

And Dylan, not being at all the fretting kind, did not fret.

As his mother said later, "He likes playing with water, so that was fine, and we managed to stand on the coal bunker outside and pass some toys through the window crack to him, and orange juice and biscuits. He is a very good mimic, so I acted out unbolting the door, and he went over to it and imitated my movements. The only thing was, he didn't actually touch the bolt, so the door stayed locked. We talked to him, of course, and he chatted back, perfectly happy."

This awkward, but unperturbing, situation continued for a little while.

Eventually, Dylan's mother concluded that some outside professional assistance was needed. She quietly called the fire brigade.

In no time, a particularly thin fireman was being fed head first through the crack in the window.

As he came through, he said, "Hullo, Dylan."

Dylan glanced up, said hullo back, and then went on playing.

The fireman unlocked the door. The fire brigade then let Dylan sit in the fire engine, and everyone had a great time.

Minutes later, a knock at the door sounded. Opened, it revealed a gentleman of the press. In answer to his questionings, this gentleman was given to understand that nothing seriously untoward had occurred—as, indeed, it had not.

But when the paper came out, it contained a small paragraph that read in part: " … firemen removed a hysterical youngster who got stuck in the lavatory … at his home … on Monday."

Now, according to my dictionary, "hysterical" means "wildly emotional." And according to the same book, "truthful" means "characterized by truth; veracious; rendering reality accurately."

Dylan's mother later happened to come across the reporter. In answer to her expressed surprise at the report, he said he felt she had not given him "enough information," so he had been forced to "create a little."

The event was little enough, certainly, but "create a little" is still an intriguing understatement to cover the difference between calm and hysterical.

Why do the media feel that emotive language is so necessary? It occurs more and more even in the most "respectable" publications.

Perhaps we should really blame Lord Northcliffe. Wasn't it this newspaper baron who observed that if a dog bites a man, it isn't news, but if a man bites a dog, *that's* news?

One gets the feeling sometimes that ever since this useful guideline was uttered, a large part of the news profession has been looking for men biting dogs, and if they are emotional about it, so much the better.

What puzzles me is that the simple facts were not felt to be interesting enough. What made Dylan's little adventure entertaining was his apparent unawareness that there was anything odd about being temporarily unable to escape from a bathroom or that a thin fireman came through the narrow window opening.

It so happens that I have inside information on another recent newsworthy incident.

This involved the teenage son of a friend. We'll call him Sebastian.

Sebastian has a pal with a metal detector. During their school vacation, the two of them detected a metal object in the school grounds. Soon afterwards, someone happened to see Sebastian walking past the notable example of 18th-century architecture that is the school's main building. He was carrying the found object.

"I think," said this person to Sebastian, "that what you are carrying is a bomb."

"You mean," asked Sebastian, just to make sure, "that this object is a bomb?"

So Sebastian put it on the ground and rapidly left the scene.

The building and grounds were evacuated. Experts came. Thin firemen and others. They confirmed that it was an unexploded German bomb from World War II. If it exploded, it would cause a notable degree of havoc.

They then proceeded to bury it under sandbags and to detonate it safely. Sebastian is going to be more careful of metal objects from now on.

The local papers reported this, of course. But what intrigued me was that only one reporter came from any *national* paper. This paper is a keen modern proponent of the "man-bites-dog" philosophy, but finally it printed nothing. My friend came to the conclusion that this was probably because nobody was hurt. And although the newspaper in question is surely no stranger to the "create-a-little" approach, its editors apparently felt that nothing could be done to this quietly resolved occurrence in the way of hysterical language to make it sufficiently alarming to attract the readers.

The excellent news that nobody was scathed and that historical buildings were preserved and that courage and quickness disarmed this dangerous hangover from the war—all this was evidently only of local interest.

Can I be forgiven for feeling that in both instances the newspapers mentioned missed fine opportunities of cheering people up? Not that one wants to *whitewash* the world. If a man sinks his eye-teeth into an unfortunate poodle, naturally I want to know all about it over breakfast. How could I get through the day if I didn't?

It's just that I wouldn't mind also knowing about people's steadiness in fearsome circumstances, or about their specific kindnesses, or their lack of prejudice, or their generosity. I want to know more about some of the things that looked as though they might go wrong—but didn't.

1987

Seashells on a Plate

I suppose I can't be the only man around who has Walter Mittyish dreams. In my case, though, they are not so much of grandeur, as of effectiveness. And I mean effectiveness in a very particular context: the Italian restaurant. Sometimes these places intimidate me.

Of course, most restaurants of any ambition aim at style. It's just that the Italians do it with such—style. They are in love with flair. The expensiveness of the restaurant has little to do with it. And it's not *what* you eat that counts so much as *how* you eat it. The client is expected to produce some approximation of urbanity. You soon know, if you go to an Italian restaurant, if you're urbane enough. And you know if you're *not*.

This was brought home to me with renewed force the other day in Notting Hill Gate.

I made three mistakes. The first was to want a meal too early in the evening. This meant that I was the sole customer in the Rigoletto Restaurant (to disguise its name). Apart from me, there were just the waiter, the waitress, and a rather stout, stationary man I took to be the proprietor. At least, he appeared to have nothing to do except propriet. I secretly named him Benvenuto.

My second mistake—though I can't exactly explain why it seemed like a mistake—was to enter the Rigoletto carrying an old canvas bag that I use as a small suitcase when away from home for a night or two. It has a tendency to bulge, and its zip is not too sure of itself. Frankly, it lacks style.

It was my third mistake, however, that made the occasion memorable—if that is the right adjective for something you'd rather forget.

The large menu arrived as if on wings. My eyes fell on the less expensive pasta. "Try something," said the voice of adventure, "you haven't tried before."

The waiter returned, *with* style. "Signor?"

It is only in private that I can imitate an Italian accent with any semblance of a semblance of accuracy. It's a mischievous habit, really, but it makes me laugh. In public, though, I hold back, and I come out very British. "I'd like— um—spaghetti er—alla von-go-le, ahem, please." And then I heard myself adding: "What is it, actually?"

The waiter succeeded in overwhelming me with the generous volubility of his one-word explanation: "Shellafeesh."

Well, I'll tell you. If you've never had the misfortune to be served *Spaghetti alla Vongole,* what it is, basically, is a scoop of rough seashore on a plate. Eating spaghetti efficiently is, at the best of times, problematical; one never quite manages to tie up the loose ends. But eating spaghetti together with a topping of deceased, crunchy, and sea-weedy shells is, as someone or other said of the Sydney Opera House, "on the edge of the impossible."

I was struck by a sense of indecision spiced with optimism. But just how *do* you eat a carapace? I wondered if perhaps all that hard clutter and clatter of shells had, after all, been rendered edible by some softening magic in the kitchen. Otherwise, why serve them up as a meal?

The sophisticated reader will, by now, have written me off as a culinary idiot. That is your right, of course. But the point was that as far as I could determine, these seashells had nothing at all inside them. It was like being served boiled eggs that contain neither yolks not whites. Nothing but shells. Whatever meat these oceanic mollusks might have once contained had long since been washed away or ingested by some passing crab.

However, a surreptitious test with the fork quickly convinced me that even if you *are* meant to chew and swallow these crustaceous substances, I, for one, was not even going to try. So how on earth does one eat this complex dish? I grabbed a roll and butter, playing for time. Then, bracing myself, I plunged into the garlicky embranglement.

The quality of *nightmare* in the experience was not in the least alleviated by the unblinking gaze of the major domo down at the other end of the restaurant. His attitude was one of supreme indifference coupled with supreme *interest.* His challenge was clear: to preserve the status and reputation of his restaurant, I must not only eat my *Spaghetti alla Vongole* hook, line, and sinker in a manner that made it perfectly evident I had eaten this dish many times before, but I must also do it with appreciative zest—*con brio*—and all the way to the finishing post. Nothing less would do.

The practical problem to be solved was simple enough: how to achieve a mouthful of sauce and pasta without also achieving a mouthful of mollusk. As I did battle, I musingly considered the sober fact that this plate piled with a clutter of cuttle-bone bore a striking resemblance to the kind of gritty stuff

Christopher Andreae

poultry men feed to chickens to toughen up their eggshells.

Just to make the obstacle course more fun, the cook had smashed up and mingled invisibly in the melee a few pieces of horny crust so that even with the most meticulous care the eater's bite might still be surprised by a sudden crunch. I should have carefully counted those tiny shards as I patiently separated and lodged them precariously on the edge of the charger. It might have soothed me.

It was a long haul. That big man watched my every move. But, finally, I drew to a halt. I'd done my best. I'd eaten not only the pasta and the sauce; I had pretended to eat all the non-existent contents of the shells too. To my relief, the dish was at last cleared. I had even begun to strike up a not unfriendly relationship with its oceanic flavor. Though I had in fact eaten very little, it strangely felt like a lot.

The waiter offered dessert. I chose the safest: fruit salad. No tricks here, I thought, nothing hard or brittle. I leant back, stretching out my legs under the small table, rather pleased with my vanquishment of the *vongole....*

"One fresh-a fruit-a salad," the waiter announced in recitative, placing it with a flourish in front of me.

"Ah, thank you," I said, man-of-the-worldishly, sitting up again. As I did so, my feet inadvertently caught the table leg, the table wobbled, and the salad lurched, throwing its juice across the cloth and all over my shirt.

Everyone—waiter, waitress, even old Benvenuto himself down there in the shadows—decided the time had come to just *ignore* me. Even I decided to ignore me. Some people should only eat at home.

But now I threw all care to the winds. I took a large, bold spoonful of fruit and bit into it.

There was a terrible crunch.

The grape in my mouth contained at least five hard seeds.

Oh, what the heck! I just smiled and swallowed the lot. Some styles of cooking are just not *meant* to be comfortable I suppose.

1980

A Little Light Praise

A little praise can sometimes go a surprisingly long way—"little" being the operative word. Too much praise may be counterproductive, even if it might be merited. Dr. Johnson, as is often the case, put it well and wittily: "Praise, like gold and diamonds, owes its value only to its scarcity."

As an Englishman living in Scotland for long enough now, surely, to have formed an opinion, I would venture to suggest that the vigorously English Dr. Johnson *must* have had some Scottish blood in him. In Scotland, praise is kept under lock and key and saved for special occasions.

Without question, Johnson would have disputed such an outrageous claim on his ancestry as even a *hint* of Scottish genealogy. And when he traveled to Scotland, although he was in the company of James Boswell, who was definitely a Scot, Johnson was not notably polite about Scots and Scotland. "But, Sir, let me tell you," he exclaimed, "the noblest prospect which a Scotchman ever sees, is the high road that leads him to England!"

I can't agree. I wouldn't (for the sake of marital harmony, if nothing else) *dare* to agree. Scots in my experience are not what caricatures of them often mindlessly report. They are not mean but extremely generous. They are not dour but very cheerful and friendly. And, by and large, when you consider some of the things we English have historically perpetrated against them, they are surprisingly nice to us.

All the same, two things I would say are true about Scots in a general way: (1) Their native language contains an electrifying affluence of percussive words and phrases designed to *insult*. (2) They really are extremely parsimonious, or at best succinct, when it comes to giving praise.

A case in point. A play I was in a while ago was seen by my wife and her aunt. I think they accompany each other to my amateur efforts on the boards out of an a kind of affectionate solidarity or an indulgence of my inexplicable descent into second childhood; but between them, they remain clear-eyed and critically sharp. They are both Scots, so one can expect from them straightforward honesty. Flattery would simply not ring true. After this particular play, when I returned home, my Best Critic, sitting up in bed with a book, offered, without much prompting, her assessment of the performance. I should explain that I had a small (if frequently entering-and-exiting) role in this play, but I convinced myself that it is indeed true that no part is a poor part, and all should be played to the full. So I was modestly enthusiastic about my wholehearted rendering of this little but busy part.

"The man in the lead role—what's his name? David?—he was very good," declared the embedded critic.

"What did you think of his hair?" I asked.

"His hair?"

"Did you realize it was a wig?"

"It *was?*"

"It was."

"Well! I'd never have guessed …. And the girl who played the tarty woman—"

"Claire."

"Ah, Claire, yes—she was the best. Really excellent. But …"

And here, in recognition of the mere milk of human kindness, I will draw a discreet veil over her astute and blunt critique of several of the other actors in the piece she felt had, well, somewhat failed to reach the highest standards. But, suffice it say, virtually no one was left entirely unscathed, and a few would have had their breakfasts ruined had they read her comments in the morning paper.

I listened and nodded and agreed and now and then defended, and finally, when she had assessed all of my fellow players, she returned to her book, one more efficient job done.

Except that her job, I couldn't help noticing, wasn't *quite* done. She had said nothing at all, whatsoever, or in the least, about *my* performance. Now I could have let the matter rest. But as Henry Ward Beecher helpfully expresses it in one of my dictionaries of quotations, "A man who does not love praise is not a full man." My hesitation, of course, resulted from the fact that I could not be sure her silence had denoted a truly Scottish reluctance to give praise. It might just as easily have meant a kindly reluctance to criticize. How could I know?

I headed for the bathroom. But then I thought, *No, I'll risk my self-respect and not let her get away with it.* So I turned round and, poking my head around the door mischievously, put her on the spot. "You had something to say about everyone in the play … except me."

She looked up. With only the most negligible intake of breath and without the slightest telltale emphasis she replied, "Oh, you were fine," and returned to her book.

This almost neutral remark left me, of course, magnificently unconvinced. I knew she couldn't (or at least I thought she couldn't) have said, "Oh, you were terrible." And I didn't expect her to say, all in one gushing breath, "Darling, you were so amazingly unmitigatedly gloriously wonderful that you should immediately audition for the National Theatre!" (There are limits even to the wildest imaginations.) But even her level-toned, entirely judicious statement was infused with an infuriating ambiguity.

In the dressing room the next day, I mentioned this wifely assessment to one of the other actors (who, truth to tell, had not come off without some not-to-be-repeated and astringent comments on her performance), and she said (being a Scot, and translating for an Englishman): "But that was *very high praise!*"

I felt better.

Then came the next play, and again I played a small character part, and again gave it everything I could muster, and again my wife and her aunt dutifully attended. And once again, my best critic was a-book and a-bed when I returned home after the performance.

"That was the most terrible, frightful, boring play ever," she said. "And the actors! You couldn't *hear* half of them. The lighting was terrible. There was no story. The jokes weren't funny. The theatre was freezing. And the play, if you can call it a play, went on and on and on. I thought it would never end.... " She paused. Then she said that her aunt's comment was "'Well ... that was ... an interesting ... experience. Tell Christopher that he was by far the best.'"

I glowed for a day and a half in the warmth of that complimentary message (even if her aunt's niece did not actually echo it).

And then it struck me. I might have been "the best," but—comparisons being odorous, as someone once said—to be "the best" only because everyone else in the play was so improbably bad, is very faint praise.

And then again I thought, *No, no. 'Praise is always pleasing, let it come from whom, or upon what account it will.'*

And I added to myself, "So if that was true for Montaigne, it is good enough for me. Enjoy the praise, my friend. All—after all—is *vanity.*"
2003

My Heart Is Merry and Bright—It's December 28

I'd like to wish you a happy Christmas.

"But it's *after* Christmas," I hear you cry.

That, however, is just the point. This is the only safe time for balanced assessment.

If I had said what I am about to say *before* Christmas—if I had cast aspersions on the annual extravaganza five days ago—it would doubtless have brought down on me dire accusations of Scroogism and wet-blanketing.

So it must be said and done off-season.

Here goes: *Christmas tree lights are a horrendous, stupendous, mind-bendous invention, without which I am firmly persuaded the universe would be a nicer and definitely sweeter place.*

It may strike the reader that I have an unreasoning dislike of something that gives innocent pleasure to trillions. So don't mistake. I like the lights, as such. In fact, I love them.

Let me convince you. We had some colored lights when I was a child that had colors you don't see nowadays. The blues were so rare and deeply opaque, so magical and gelatinously, truly blue that the burning filament within scarcely managed to escape visibly. Only a completely darkened drawing room made it possible to really see that blue: the blue of intense dreams. It was wonderful. The yellow and the orange lights were deliciously the color and translucency of Rowntree's Fruit Gums, and for all I know may well have tasted similarly citric if licked. The red lights were thick and heavy with regal mystique; the green … it was one of those greens you see if you close your eyes and think *GREEN!*

These lights were meant to be approximately flame shaped but were more like small fruit. They were glorious, had a distinct kind of hot smell when lit, and are now inextricably connected in my memory corridors with the spiky aroma of the tree itself and with a marvelous collection of old-fashioned tree decorations, which it became my entirely pleasurable childhood duty to hang on the tree each year. These consisted of sugary balls, with shells thinner than thrushes' eggs, suspended in gold filigree; a yellow glass canary in a glass cage; papier-mâché birds—bullfinches and blue tits—that clipped on the branches; thin, limp strands of tinsel (for icicles), astonishingly weighty by today's standards (what were they made of I wonder—shredded lead?).

No decorations and no lights I've come across since have been close to those childhood ones. And it must be said that the lights were not only unforgettable in color, they were also very *reliable.*

They were made by a manufacturer who saw them as a valuable, once-in-a-lifetime purchase. Every year I'd unbox them without any doubt that they would instantly light. The wires between the bulbs were sturdily made. The screw-in sockets were crafted with care and precision out of durable metal. The glass of the bulbs was rock solid. The filaments were immovable and shockproof.

Today, I actually dread the imminence of the festive season because I know that, once again, I shall be locked in deadly conflict with the Christmas lights. We have several sets amounting to, I don't know, a thousand or so bulbs—little colored lights, programmed with mind-boggling ingenuity to flash on and off in any number of sequences; a set of white twinklers; an array of little white sparkles. All of these lights, in their different ways, are the source of tribulation and anxiety. They are *entirely* unpredictable. They can cease working, either altogether, or in sporadic, incomprehensible, flickering groupings of seven or 15 or 26.

Europe, a few years back, did not seem to have discovered little white lights for *outdoor* use. Only very large and usually colored bulbs were weatherproof enough for that. Little twinklers were for indoors, safe from the weather. So my wife and I started out by importing outdoor ones from unsuspecting friends in the United States. These lights required voltage transformers. With some strings of lights, things are so engineered that if one goes out, the others stay lit. Not these. One burns out; they *all* go out.

All too frequently, I have stood shivering and drenched trying to find out which nasty little bulb is the guilty party. I needn't explain the mathematical enormity of the problem of trying out 100 little bulbs to find one dud. And these bulbs are the push-in type: You shove hard. They snap, or twist, or break, or shatter. You run out of spares. The stores are shut for the holidays. It is such fun.

Then finally, three winters ago, there was a further blow. Our upstairs neighbor appeared on the scene with his portable radio. "Whenever your lights are on," he observed, "I can't hear my music."

"It's only about ten days," I said, "and only at night."

"But I like listening to my music for ten days at night," he not entirely unreasonably replied.

That was when we discovered that the Germans had started making little white outdoor lights. And the transformer *they* supplied did not interfere with radios. So we ditched our American lights and settled for Deutschland uber alles. I assumed my troubles were over.

Between Christmas 1988 and Christmas 1989, the two sets of German lights, 40 bulbs a set, had rested untouched in the basement. But when I plugged them in, I discovered they had only a total of eleven bulbs that lit. I unapologetically threw the lot in the trash bin.

Then I took them out again and drove to the garden center from which we had unwittingly bought them a year before.

There we complained, and bought two more sets, and received promises of recompense and seasonal goodwill. We waited for a calm, dry December night to put the lights on the outside tree. No such night came, so we put them up on a bitter, pouring, blasterous December night instead.

While still in their box, every bulb had shone. Now, on the tree, two didn't. Next morning, five didn't. By the next night, eight had gone. I reached for the spares—only three per set. A total of three of these spares turned out to be non-operational. I drove back to the garden centre, and they—amid protestations of recompense and seasonal goodwill to all men and in particular us—sold us more bulbs from the only set they had left. Note the word "sold."

Well—they lit. And they stayed lit. They were, I willingly admit, an unmitigated delight. Everybody who passed, admired. We admired. Then Christmas was over. It's a quick event. I waited for a calm dry January night to take them off the tree. So I took them off in February. It was too late. The latest wind-storm had torn through them with disastrous effect. Wires were broken, bulbs shattered, little fragments of German engineering were found during the ensuing months in different extremities of the garden.

So now I simply dare not plug them in to see what happens. I know what won't happen, anyway. If I'm fortunate, one or two will light up. But realistically I expect darkness.

Tell me. Should I really feel merry and bright? *Should* I?

1990

Hearts to You

First warning. This article is not for those of innocent years or of a disposition inclined toward romantic vapor.

It will contain such emotive words (probably misspelled) as coochicoo and tiddlums, not to mention cuddlypoos and snooklesberry. It speaks of hearts and flowers (though, incidentally, I personally prefer chocolates). It speaks of love. It speaks of our kitchen.

Our kitchen might well be included in the *Guinness Book of World Records.* It runs along the lines of how many college students of average size but extraordinary squeezability can simultaneously co-inhabit a phone box. But in this case it is about hearts—how many hearts can a kitchen contain?

This kitchen of ours has more hearts in it than I have had hot dinners. There are bowls decorated with friezes of hearts. There are refrigerator magnets sporting hearts. There are mobiles that are heart-shaped or star-shaped with numerous hearts incorporated therein. There are cutout hearts collaged to walls and cupboard doors—hearts like balloons with small pandas hanging onto their strings, hearts surmounted by tigers, hearts with cats silhouetted against them as if gazing at the moon.

There is a miniature shopping bag containing a creature of ursine aspect and the words "kiss, kiss" on the outside, with hearts instead of dots over the "i's." Three white birds fly in the center of a red heart hanging by a thread from the ceiling. Suspended over the glass of the back door is another heart in which a white duck pulls a smaller white duck in a wagon. And then there is an apron hanging on a hook. At first sight, you might think its all-over decoration consists of flowers. On second look, you see that these "flowers" are actually hearts—and there are hundreds of them.

"What," I asked nonchalantly of my spouse, "is the meaning of all these hearts throughout our kitchen space?"

"I don't know, really," she replied, just as nonchalantly. "It could be because the decor of the kitchen is red and white." It was not *precisely* the answer I had expected, but then you can't have everything.

Second warning. This next part of my article is *shocking* and should be skipped by readers who do not wish to be disenchanted. Nevertheless, in the interests of veracity, I should quote an appropriate definition from my encyclopedia—*Webster's New World,* that is: "Valentine, St. According to tradition a bishop of Terni martyred at Rome, now omitted from the calendar of saints' days as probably nonexistent. His festival was Feb. 14, but the custom of sending 'valentines' to a loved one on that day seems to have arisen because the day accidentally coincided with the Roman mid-February festival of Lupercalia." And: "Lupercalia. Roman festival celebrated Feb. 15. It took place at the Lupercal, the cave where Romulus and Remus were supposedly suckled by the wolf (lupus). Lupercalia included feasting, dancing and sacrificing goats ...."

Over the dubious and legendary history of Romulus, Remus, and the She-Wolf, I prefer to draw a veil, except to note in passing that of all the protagonists in that somewhat grisly tale, Mrs. Wolf, I feel, comes out head and shoulders above everyone else for sheer generosity of attitude and high character.

Third warning. Arguably this next section of my essay is even more shocking. It concerns the practice of sending valentines.

Not forgetting what the careless sending of an anonymous valentine can cause in the way of mischief (see Thomas Hardy's *Far From the Madding Crowd*), and apart from the fact that my wife always receives at least one such card on which the heavily disguised handwriting looks suspiciously familiar to me, I will admit for the very first time in the public domain to having dispatched—as a callow youth—one valentine that until recently I could hardly have mentioned without a sharp touch of embarrassment.

I was still in school. So was the recipient of my card. I had met her at a school dance. We sang, as we danced (prompted I assume by the band), "Daddy Wouldn't Buy Me a Bow-Wow." It was this significant and profoundly unromantic line that I inscribed with trembling fingers inside the card. I slipped it daringly into its envelope and then, even more courageously, I mailed it.

I *desperately* hoped she would guess who had sent it. I *desperately* hoped she would *not* guess who had sent it. I *desperately* wished I had not sent it. I was *desperately* pleased that I had. For days I wondered if she had received it. For days I wondered if she had guessed who sent it.

Twenty years later, I met the mother of this schoolgirl at an adult summer school. I was a teacher. The girl's mother was a student.

Sitting down to lunch next to this "student" who knows so much more about everything than I do, I suddenly found she was introducing me to her daughter. "This is my daughter, Lady Blank. She's visiting me at the moment. I don't suppose you have met? She has been living abroad. Sir Blank Blank, her husband, is in the diplomatic service." Lady Blank looked, well—blank. She also looked scrupulously elegant. As far as I could see, she did not have a bow-wow. Clearly she had no clue at all who I might be.

"Well," I said, "in fact we did meet once."

"We did?" she said, taking a neat bite of her shepherd's pie. "When?"

"Well," I said, "you were at school. And I was a school. We met at a school dance."

"Did we?" she said.

"Yes," I said. "Now don't laugh. But I sent you a valentine card. I never knew if you received it."

She popped a tidy sprout in her mouth. "How very nice of you," she said. *How very diplomatic of* you, I thought.

Final warning. This section brings everything out in the open in the most shameful way. Last year the *Times* (of London) printed, as it usually does, a page full of Valentine's Day messages, alphabetically arranged. Here are some of my favorites:

Pickle. You always got me into one, but I love you anyway. Will you dine with me tonight?

Felicity. You are the best thing since sliced bread. Dave.

I'm told that happiness is being in love with a Welsh Woman. I think it's true. Mothy.

Dearest Cuddlypoos. With all my love at the start of our new life together.

Kissyface. Another year and it's even better. Yours forever, Buttons.

To Shiny. My funny Valentine. For always with my love, your wife.

What puzzles me about such messages is that they are, so to speak, so vulnerably *public*.

I mean—what if Cuddlypoos turns out to be someone else with the same name? Or what if Kissyface takes another paper besides the *Times*? And where is the embarrassment factor in society today, when someone will admit in a national newspaper, in open and full view of all prying and curious eyes, to being called *Mothy*?

We live in a strange world.

There was, however, one message on the page that really caught my eye and held it:

Christopher. You are my little favourite. I love you so much.

So? Is there a law against taking things personally? What I'd like to say in response is this:

Snugglepot. The same to you. Meet me in the kitchen?
1994

XI.
Reading, Writing, Listening, and Looking

Potter Cried "Bosh!"

"Never does anyone outside your perfidiously complimentary nation write to tell me that I write good prose."

But Miss Bertha Mahony (who had founded The Bookshop for Boys and Girls in Boston in 1916) had written to that effect, and Beatrix Potter—author, after all, as well as artist-illustrator of her "little books" for children—was pleased enough by the compliment to put down on paper for Miss Mahony some thoughts about her way of writing.

She enjoyed writing she said, so she took pains over it. She disliked writing to order but preferred to please herself. "My usual way of writing," she went on, "is to scribble, and cut out, and write it again and again. The shorter and plainer the better. And read the Bible (unrevised version and Old Testament) if I feel my style wants chastening."

It's a craftsman's analysis, typically blunt and unpretentious. Potter *was* unpretentious. In fact, if there is a common theme to just about everything she wrote, it might be the deflation of pretension.

The same was true with her pictures. She cried "Bosh!" when someone tried to fit her art into the English tradition of landscape painting that included such greats as Samuel Palmer and John Constable. She wasn't just being modest (as some of her devotees think); she was quite right. She isn't in their league. She greatly admired Constable and knew that her meticulous and delightful illustrations didn't come (or try to come) remotely into the same category. She knew exactly what art had influenced her, though, and said so: the pre-Raphaelites and the fruit-and-flower pieces of William Henry Hunt.

But what she liked about American reactions to her writing, and her books as a whole, was not merely the praise, but the fact that Americans took children's literature seriously. It mattered to them that it should be good. It wasn't just trivial toy making.

Potter seemed to feel her fellow Englishmen refused to be as serious about it—though perhaps she wasn't being entirely fair. Her books were remarkably popular in her native land, and not, surely, even initially, with children only. Like many children's classics, they can have an almost greater attraction to grown-ups than to the smaller people for whom they are purportedly written.

Though her books are physically constructed to be held by small children, they nevertheless often seem to have been written with the assumption that they would be read to the child by an adult. Potter's language, her memorable phrases, the development of her narratives, her prose, with its cadences and rhythm, love of alliteration, onomatopoeia, and choice of the apt word, were all undoubtedly part of her appeal to adults. Although she had immediate rapport with children, she actually wrote *as* an adult. Her manner of writing so often carries undertones of rather subtle irony; her tone of voice continually breaks through; and her vocabulary, in particular, is spiced with such deliberately adult words as *soporific, affronted, resourceful, disdainful,* and (in a wonderful sentence in *Jemima Puddle-Duck)* the word *superfluous.*

"Jemima," we read, "complained of the superfluous hen"—the hen, that is, who had been employed to hatch her eggs because she was such "a bad sitter." Jemima, in her poke bonnet and shawl (ducks look daft in clothes particularly if they are out of fashion), you can be reasonably certain, would not have herself used the word *superfluous,* any more than a child would; after all, as Potter observes with characteristic directness and justice, her heroine (?) was a "simpleton."

In 1933, a highly regarded novelist—an Englishman—did write an essay for the *London Mercury* in which he gave considered attention to Potter as a writer. This was Graham Greene. His essay has just been republished in *The Hutchinson Book of Essays.*

Greene strikes a balance, in this assessment of Potter the writer, between humor and indubitable admiration. If he compares her with E. M. Forster, with Henry James, and even finally with Shakespeare (in terms of her development from comedy via near-tragedy to her final *"Tempest," Little Pig Robinson*), he does so with his tongue only slightly in his cheek and is making as much fun of these writers as he is of her. (The only problem with Greene's essay is that he overlooked the fact that *Little Pig Robinson* was not her final work at all; published as the last of her little books in 1930, it was actually one of the first stories she had written.)

In fact, as his autobiography notes, Greene has himself on several occasions echoed Potter in his own writings, and he suggests that H. G. Wells did likewise at least once.

Greene also concluded, from the way in which her books became more pessimistic, that "some time between 1907 and 1909, Miss Potter must have passed through an emotional ordeal which changed the character of her genius.… " Something "happened that shook [her] faith in appearance."

As a response to Greene's essay, once again Potter cried "Bosh!" and the rather "acid" letter Greene received from her apparently indicated no appreciation of Greene's appreciation, which is a great pity because it was genuine and basically serious. She denied his "emotional disturbance" theory, and "she deprecated sharply 'the Freudian school' of criticism," Greene notes. Nevertheless, the fact is that she *had* gone through a difficult period—though it was earlier than Greene's dates—when her fiancé had suddenly died. Maybe this affected the tone of her work, maybe not. What Greene, however, overlooks is that Beatrix Potter really had *never* had "faith in appearance." Her stories had said precisely that from the start, over and over again.

The symbol she had used was dress.

In an essay first published last year, "The Subversive Element in Beatrix Potter," Humphrey Carpenter examines Potter's writing in great depth. He continually, among many other illuminating points, refers in passing to Potter's use of clothes as "symbols of social pretension."

Carpenter might possibly have emphasized this as a more central theme, a real issue in her writing. Perhaps he didn't because in this aspect of her many-layered tales, it is not possible to separate the writing from the pictures, and he was concentrating on her writing. But after all, the ingenious interdependence between image and word is one of her tales' chief delights: it is almost a dialogue in itself. It is hard to know which is more important— pictures or writing.

Without the space here to detail it, I would recommend a study of the Potter Tales from the *clothes* point of view—from Peter Rabbit losing his under Mr. McGregor's gate, via Mrs. Tiggy-Winkle washing just about everybody's, to Tom Kitten's bursting buttons, to Thomasina Tittlemouse's Christmas present for rescuing the Flopsy Bunnies (enough rabbit wool for a cloak, hood, muff, and mittens).

Potter's favorite story, *The Tailor of Gloucester,* which many commentators have isolated from the others as being quite different, falls centrally into place when considered as another, indeed primary, story about the symbolic character of clothes. What her animal characters wear or don't wear (and when) is crucial: it's what makes them, one might say, "human"—

since that is precisely the chief fantasy, (humor, absurdity, and meaning) of her stories.

Potter's journal shows conclusively how fascinated she was by clothes and what they indicate about people in them. She was particular in her tales about appropriateness of dress—or about judging the right time in a story for animals to return to a state of nature, unclothed. She had very particular notions of what was appropriate, and what was not, in the fictional humanizing of animals. She criticized Kenneth Grahame, author of *The Wind in the Willows*, for allowing Toad to have hair. Galoshes (which her Jeremy Fisher wears, and a macintosh, which saves his life) are permissable; but frogs and toads don't have hair, and that's that.

One or two of her stories, it is true, are not concerned with clothes at all—*Squirrel Nutkin* for instance; but most are, and they are mainly the "comedies." By the time of her late "near-tragedy," *The Tale of Mr. Tod*, her pictures still show her characters (two of them extremely "disagreeable")—in clothes, but the words don't mention them. Her "people-animals" have now virtually become "animal-animals." The threatening, savage side of nature—which was always there under the pretense and make-believe in the earlier tales—is fully out in the open.

This change paralleled her life. She had gradually freed herself from the suffocating demands and assumptions of her upper-middle class parents and gained independence. She also escaped from the city. And in the country, she did something other than write fairy tales about dressed-up animals. She *farmed*—with real animals. She found that working with real animals took away her fantasies about storybook animals.

Pictures of Potter as a farmer in the Lake District in the last happy 30 years of her life show a distinct lack of concern for niceties of attire. Such societal signifiers had become largely "superfluous." Like the independent Peter, she had squeezed under the symbolic gate in her determination to escape captivity and pretension. Unless, of course, such a notion is altogether too—*Freudian.*

1990

Legible Characters

I'm not entirely sure when Charles Dodgson wrote his *Eight or Nine Wise Words About Letter Writing*, but I'm sure he wrote it in a very clear hand. After all, he was a mathematician, so presumably he had the same respect for readable letters that he had for unmistakable numbers.

His Golden Rule for letter writers was: "Write legibly."

Dodgson (better known by his pen name, Lewis Carroll) went on a bit about this rule.

"The average temper of the human race," he suggested, "would be perceptibly sweetened, if everybody obeyed this Rule! ... Years ago, I used to receive letters from a friend—and very interesting letters too—written in one of the most atrocious hands ever invented. It generally took me about a week to read one of his letters. I used to carry it about in my pocket, and take it out at leisure times, to puzzle over the riddles which composed it—holding it in different positions, and at different distances, till at last the meaning of some hopeless scrawl would flash upon me, when I at once wrote down the English under it; and, when several had been thus guessed, the context would help with the others, till at last the whole series of hieroglyphics was deciphered."

I don't believe my dad ever read this advice. But at least he was aware that his handwriting presented a degree of puzzlement to others.

When I was away at boarding school, he and my mother wrote to me every week with devoted regularity. She wrote her letters in a unique cursive, curly style all her own. Her words were permed. I could read her letters easily, but then I had been born to it.

My dad didn't write his letters. He typed them. He did so, not out of formality or because he wanted to instill in his hopelessly unbusinesslike son a sense of the significance of The Business Letter, but because he knew for certain that I would be unable to interpret a single word otherwise.

I did occasionally catch a glimpse of his handwriting, and it seemed to consist mostly of horizontal lines that trembled and twitched now and then as if recording some very minor seismic disturbance. In the main, it just streaked along the paper from left to right (presumably) like a spider at dawn leaving a trail in dew. There were little jumps above the line, and occasional tails dangling below the line, but any other indication of actual *words* was not easy to determine.

The first headmaster I encountered was a remarkable, fine, intellectual man, and he similarly had an appallingly obscure way with pen and ink. But instead of resorting to an Olivetti, he—as if he were taking a solemn vow— suddenly resolved to reform his handwriting completely.

I remember this turn of events with the same childish amazement and admiration I felt at the time. He had, like all adults, always struck me as someone who knew everything and did all things superlatively. It simply hadn't entered my thought that he might feel he had something to learn. We were pupils. He was teacher. He was the instiller—we the instilled.

He taught himself Italic script. He invested in a special pen with a special nib. He practiced, with all due thickness and thinness, with all due forward lean, and with all due regard for upward strokes and downward strokes, the formation and finesse of individual letters. Then he turned to the question of how to make these newly acquired characters touch fingers and walk together across the paper in a natural flow but still with no loss of clarity.

I was at an age when each week saw a new experiment with my own handwriting. I think I was trying hard to make it all into a kind of endless signature, different from everyone else's. I had the idea that this would make it very grown-up. After all, it hadn't been many years since I'd started to form letters of any sort. I was still a beginner.

But observing a highly respected teacher of incalculable age and achievements learning to write all over again as if he were a five-year-old, presented me with an immensely persuasive model. Naturally, I started to imitate.

The headmaster's new Italics became the basis of my own hand. A teacher much later in my schooldays even saw fit to give me a writing prize. This took me by utter surprise and was greeted with a mix of incredulity and laughter by classmates. Even the teacher felt his decision needed explanation. He said my writing "had character." He never mentioned legibility. I suspect, in fact, he meant me to be a kind of grenade thrown into the path of those boys who wrote with painstaking neatness. By then my writing had become impassioned, hasty, wild—even, one might say, *driven*. But at least it wasn't boring.

What has happened to it since is probably best described as calligraphic erosion. Edges have softened. Sharps have become flats. Some words have gone floppy in the middle. Ends trail. Am I becoming the son of my father? I have developed loose habits with words ending in "-ing." My lowercase v's, r's, and s's are often distinguishable only by context. My n's and u's are clones of each other. In short, my handwriting grows curiouser and curiouser.

Yet underneath it all, still lies a headmaster and his marvelous resolution. This memory, in fact, brings me up short quite often, and I severely tell myself to write legibly. As if I were writing to Mr. Dodgson. (Though perhaps it'd be safer to e-mail him.)

2002

To Be Outwardly Inward

"He was always, in however broadly comic a role, a reserved and private man on stage, as if he had just wandered on, unaware that he was being observed. In none of his performances was his own secrecy ever violated."

The words are part of a recent tribute by an English writer called David Hare to an actor called Paul Dawkins in a newspaper called the *Guardian*. I am not conscious of having seen Paul Dawkins act, but no description of an actor could more tantalizingly make me wish I had. How can a man preserve *secrecy* in an art that is in its very nature outward, open, exposing, and even extrovert? Acting—performance of any sort—would seem to be such a public act as to obliterate the slightest possibility of privacy or reserve. And yet....

I once attended a concert given by a young French pianist who had recently come in second at an international music competition. She had come in *second*—not first. Perhaps the judges had been looking for that extra flair, that brilliant virtuosity that she had not quite produced.

Oddly, I have no recollection now of the program of her recital. But what I cannot forget is her quality as a *performer*—though the word is a complete distortion and diminution of what she did on the stage.

She brought onto it a profoundly quiet atmosphere. She approached the instrument with a deliberate unpretentiousness, an almost matter-of-fact manner. She might have been a weaver at the loom or a carpenter at his bench. I thought of the writer or painter who (generally) works alone, unseen, and whose art is very rarely witnessed by others during its making but seen at one remove.

She used no audience-arresting mannerism, nothing visual to catch the attention, no antics. The piano was a tool of which she had a perfect understanding. She had set up an efficient, working relationship with it. The piano was not, itself, I felt, the main point of her concentration, any more than the typewriter is for the writer. As with the actor, she seemed unaware of her audience, wrapped in the act of music, she herself listening, almost in contemplation.

This was music making freed from all show and display. It was a giving that was intensely unselfconscious and therefore, quite naturally, intensely expressive. The pianist's name is Anne Queffelec. She should have come first at this music competition—at *any* music competition (in my opinion!).

Recently, it has been dawning on me gently that I have much to perceive in this area of unassertive assertion, of statement from the center of what *is*, rather than exaggeration from the center of what I want to be. Of course, there is a legitimate strand of expressionism in art that calls for projection, overstatement, declamation. But I have, I think, felt suspicious of outwardness because it can too easily become untrue—a pretending, a disguise, or merely an impressive display of technique—while inwardness and introspection are in danger of being lost or spoiled if turned, literally, inside out.

On the other hand, it is undoubtedly the case that no artist can actually afford to see his privacy as something suppressed and without expression. What is deeply held in an individual—what deeply *belongs*—should be deeply invulnerable. I'd go further and say that by its very nature it *is* invulnerable. So its expression needs somehow to convey this. It needs to be an inwardness making itself evident without falsifying that inwardness. It is this that makes sharing possible in solitude. It is this that enables the invisible to be revealed in a painting, the inaudible heard in a voice, and secrecy contained in a performance that is, nevertheless, generously expressive.

1979

Lot Number 179

It was not so much the question itself, but what was taken for granted by the question.

"So what do you collect?"

The questioner was a dealer in Oriental antiques at an antiques fair. I wondered what lay behind his assumption that everyone collects something? Experience? Hopefulness?

His question caught me off guard.

When it comes to collecting, I believe quite firmly in the left hand not knowing what the right hand is doing. I've never admitted to being a collector, even to myself. Could this be a sign of an uneasy conscience?

But in reply, I heard myself say, "Well—bottles."

"Ah," he said, "18th-century bottles with seals?"

"More 19th without," I said. "I'm not, you see, a wealthy man," I added. "In fact, I'm a journalist, a feature writer."

I felt this revelation (or confession, if you prefer) ought to scotch any lurking optimism he might have been harboring that I was about to buy one of his minuscule boxwood Japanese carvings with their majuscule price tags. He appeared to accept fate gracefully.

"Collecting is a terrible thing," I observed. "Once it starts, it never stops. Buy one bottle, and you've got to get another to go with it. Bottles are so lonely alone. In fact, bottles are happier in hundreds."

He agreed. "*Terrible*. Collectors are people out of all control, self-abandoned, inveterate, possessed, obsessed.... They should be nipped in the bud."

On the other hand ... collecting is, after all, an investment. A hedge against inflation. A pension fund. One day, there will be a sale: assets realized, an astonishing fortune made, and astounding increases in value over years.

That's it! Collecting is reasonable. Collecting is fine.

There is a little snag, of course. It is this: I'd sooner have leaky shoes and a tattered raincoat—I might even be willing to go without a boiled egg at breakfast—rather than part with my dearly loved, frequently pored-over, proudly shared collector's items. The catch is that collectors collect things they love to have. Such things cost money to get, of course; but to *part* with them for something as crass, as meaningless, as disloyal as mere money is a fearsome and gargantuan disgrace!

Talking of tattered raincoats, I saw a few this morning at the auction of watercolors and prints in Edinburgh.

I have attended auctions before—a teddy-bear auction, an art-school auction, and one auction of house contents held in a Yorkshire marketplace. But I have never actually *bid* at an auction. I haven't dared. All these bidders—who are they? Japanese squillionaires. Yuppies. Oil magnates. Art dealers. Mums and Dads. Not *feature writers*.

But this morning all my self-depreciation was swept aside. I would boldly go! The plan was definite. I would bid for Lot 179.

Catalogs regularly arrive in the mail of upcoming auctions to be staged by Phillips Scotland. I scrupulously scan every lot (the least I can do). But never once—among all the oils and clocks, mustard pots and rugs, printed books, boxes of tinted glassware, walnut tea trays, maps and dolls and postcards—has one single item made me actually want to own and keep it.

Until this sale. Until Lot 179.

I quote: "179. BLAIR HUGHES STANTON. *The Hand*, Wood Cut, signed, inscribed, and numbered 2/20, Unframed, 24cm X 14cm and another Wood Cut by Agnes Miller Parker of a squirrel on pine tree. (2) 30-50."

I'm aware that the appeal of this lot may not be immediately apparent to others. But Stanton and Parker are two of the most notable and admired wood engravers (Phillips should know they didn't make "Wood Cuts") in 20th-century Britain. Stanton, whose work is somewhat fantastical or surreal, I can take or leave. But I wouldn't mind at all having an original impression of an Agnes Miller Parker wood engraving. And this squirrel is immaculately observed and superbly rendered.

The auction began at 11:00.

Lining the walls was an array of what seemed to me minor watercolors in tawdry frames, some 157 of them. Not terribly inspiring, I felt, but the place was full. Bidding was energetic. Some items went rapidly but others only after the auctioneer's head had almost wagged itself off his shoulders by persistently to-ing and fro-ing between somewhat disengaged competitors.

No Tokyo tycoons here today, however. Instead, middle-aged men with

Brylcreemed hair and loud, tweed jackets; county women with Queen Elizabeth headscarves; and characters—yes!—really and truly *in* tatty raincoats and leaky footwear. They were all bidding three figures for items like *A Fairy by Moonlight* or *In an Arabian Doorway* painted in 1889.

It seemed to take forever to plow through these washy old works. When we'd arrived at the saleroom, my wife had observed, "I hope this isn't going to be boring." She soon found it was, and after admonishing me not to raise even a tip of a finger by mistake, she left, preferring to go and buy some pillowcases.

The auctioneer seemed terribly sleepy (in need of pillowcases with pillows in them), as uninspired by his minor triumphs as I was by the watercolors.

But I studied form. These bidders were clearly habitués, and the minimal nonchalance with which they made their purchases was entirely admirable. A catalog would be momentarily lifted with absent-minded disinterest, and once the auctioneer on high had noticed this discreet sign, all that was needed to stay in the race was the merest suggestion of an eyelid-flutter or a barely perceptible inclination of the chin. If the price reached too high for a particular bidder, the slightest sideways motion of the head indicated a bow out.

Since I had never even thought of bidding at an auction before, I had no previous acquaintance with such subtle theatrics. Nor had I taken into account such things as commission bids and telephone bids. But now I began to notice how the auctioneer announced he could start bidding at a certain figure, or a member of the staff would bid on behalf of some absent, but usually rather determined, person.

Sometimes the estimate in the catalog for a given item would be about right. Once or twice, it was slightly too low or high. On one occasion, it was hundreds of pounds too low.

Almost two hours strolled by, and then, at last, we arrived at the final lot in the watercolor section. By now, a brusque female auctioneer had taken over, and the pace had sharpened.

This lot was obviously the star watercolor of the sale, the climax. And then we were into the prints. Now I started watching the figures carefully, noting how they varied from the estimates. Most of them were more or less on the nail. But then an etching by the Swedish artist Anders Zorn climbed merrily to 850 pounds over a top estimate of 300; and the experts got it even more wrong with a batch of large engravings after Nicolas Poussin. The estimate was 100 to 200. The final price was 1,300.

At long last, my lot was rapidly approaching.

I made two firm decisions.

First, I would on no account go over 80 pounds. I felt this was generous, given the top estimate of 50.

Second, I would bid with my left hand raised dramatically high to make very sure that the hasty podiumed lady couldn't miss seeing me.

This was my carefully conceived plan. Once I had caught the auctioneer's attention, I would bid by curt nods, as if I was an old hand at this game. I envisaged that once I had started to bid, and as the scarcely convincing competitors' bids and mine climbed to the point where my final, unchallengeable bid of 80 pounds would outstrip all rivals, and the hammer would clonk down in my favor, the hall would fall silent in admiration at the boldness and unwavering conviction of this newcomer who obviously knew a thing or two about these wood engravings.

Lot 176 … Lot 177 … Lot 178 …

I admit it: a pounding of heart there was as the lady auctioneer briskly announced: *"Lot 179."*

She looked down at her desk.

"Yes," she remarked, as if it was the most normal and natural thing in the world, "I have a commission bid for this lot and can start the bidding at— *150.…* "

So it was that I came away empty-handed. The squirrel had escaped before I chased it.

I emerged into the sunlight of George Street to find my wife just returning with pillowcases. To her questioning glance, I replied by laughing. For an hour or two, at intervals, I went on laughing and chuckling at the thought of the final bathos that had crowned my lengthy but inexpensive morning.

I had been at a hunt but nowhere near the kill. In a strange way, I felt rather good about it. Disappointment can be oddly satisfactory.

Perhaps, I concluded, bidding is more exciting than buying. Perhaps *not* bidding is more exciting than bidding. Perhaps the best thing about auctions is staying away from them.

In the car home, my wife, for no apparent reason, told me about a fellow teacher at her school who had one day seen a neighbor's droopy-eared pet rabbit.

"Oh, I'd love to have a droopy-eared rabbit!" she had exclaimed.

Some days later, this woman discovered her husband constructing something with wood and nails. It was a rabbit hutch. She was horrified.

"I had to explain to him," she told my wife, "that when I had said I'd love to have a rabbit, I didn't really *mean* I actually wanted to *own* one. I only meant—I'd 'love to have one.' That's all."

Now there's a particularly fine distinction—a hair's breadth distinction—in this, but I sort of know what she was saying. And I wondered if collectors aren't sometimes like that.

What we enjoy most is the *feeling of wanting* to collect some particular thing. The discovery, the research, the stalking, the competing, and the capture—that's the best part.

But somehow, once the object is home and dry, in the hand, possessed at last, it unaccountably loses a certain … luster. Could it be the luster that the dream of ownership lent it?

1990

The Mouse for All Seasons

Happening the other day to stroll past the Disney Store that has taken up residence in one of our shopping malls here in Glasgow, I couldn't help noticing an extremely small boy standing just outside its wide entrance. There must have been a parent nearby, but for the moment he seemed by himself. He was completely still, entranced and absorbed. And he was talking, quietly. It's noisy around there—and he wasn't audible to me.

But the Disney attendant, wearing her short outfit and obligatory smile, was watching him with real pleasure: he was so utterly engrossed, so intense and serious, so busy.

I'd like to bet that he was either talking about, or actually to, Mickey Mouse.

Since I am one of the many non-cartoon characters around who are younger than Mickey Mouse (born 1928), I never knew a world without him in it—just as this small boy will never know a world without computers and videotape. I find it a challenging act of the imagination to think that Abraham Lincoln, Queen Victoria, Dr. Johnson, Alfred the Great—indeed anyone who lived before 1928— had such terribly deprived childhoods. Who was available for *them* to talk to?

Actually, I had a small and essentially private thrill recently, when my wife dragged me to Euro Disney and there, suddenly crossing a bridge, came the real, three-dimensional, living-and-moving Mickey, accompanied by *his* other half. Never for a moment did I suspect there might be two quite ordinary (though admittedly little) humans somewhere inside; it was unimaginable. I reverted instantly to childhood and couldn't keep my eyes off the redoubtable duo. By now they had crossed to our side and were jauntily striding through the crowd as if their presence were the most unexceptional thing in the world.

But here I have to make a small confession. Although Mickey was as much a part of my childhood as anyone's, I remember wondering why it was that he spoke a *foreign language*. I could never understand a single word that came out of his expressive and perfectly circular face. I don't suppose British children today would have a similar problem, reared as they are on American TV and on pop songs that are always sung in American, even by people from Liverpool or Stockholm. My wife teaches youngsters, and she says that although they speak with profound Glasgow accents, they sing, as a matter of course, in American.

My difficulty with Mickey, I presume, was that he didn't speak like the King or a BBC announcer. If I had trouble with Mickey, it was much worse with the appalling duck, and with loose-limbed Pluto. I could, indeed, sit through an entire Mickey Mouse short film and not grasp a single cogent utterance.

In the interest of research and the checking of memories, I went into the Disney Store to find out if they had a video of a Mickey Mouse short. I wanted to know whether or not I still find the mouse for all seasons incomprehensible.

Astoundingly, given Mickey's continuing popularity, the smiling youth I summoned to my assistance thought they only had one. It was on a tape that was mainly *Peter and the Wolf*. To fill up extra space, two shorts were appended. The first was a "Silly Symphony," which involved Mickey only as the named "presenter." The second was "Symphony Hour," with Mickey as the star. I'm not sure when this little comedy was made, but the date didn't matter for my investigative purposes unless the cartoon happened to be more recent than the ones I watched as a child. I didn't want an upmarketed mouse with a voice spoken by some classically trained actor of our period. I wanted the garbled tones of the Original Rodent, possibly spoken by Walt Disney himself. He, in fact, originated the Mickey voice, and continued to dub his small, successful friend for many years.

From this short I learned two things: that at least one Mickey Mouse film has almost no speech by our hero in it at all (his only words, which I understood without difficulty, are: "Yes, Sir, Mr. Macaroni!" and "Goofy!"); and the other is that the reason there could occasionally be such a dearth of vociferation is really because Mickey's essence has far more to do with *action* than with words.

Sound, nevertheless, is an integral part of the history of Mickey Mouse, since one of the very earliest Mickey shorts was the first animated film with a fully coordinated soundtrack. And sound is central to "Symphony Hour," in which the mouse is an orchestral conductor: "Ma-estro Michel Mouse approaches the podium...." Mickey shows himself to be a mime artist of supreme ability, his white-gloved hands running the gamut of emotions, his face expressing each change of mood in the music. This famous mouse doesn't really need speech, which is probably why I loved him years ago even though he spoke so funnily.

Does this Disney character misrepresent mice? Undoubtedly he does. A real mouse is about as far from being like Mickey (who is really just two large circles, two smaller circles, with some bits and pieces added) as liberty is from being a tall lady with a torch. Mickey is a child, a little man, a straight man. He is an actor, a dreamer, ready to impersonate, like Walter Mitty, anyone from Charles Lindberg to Gulliver, from Uncle Tom to Fred Astaire, from a taxi driver to a sorcerer's apprentice to a circus ringmaster. He has aspirations to heroism yet is generally foiled in his ambitions by either circumstances or a duck.

In "Symphony Hour," it is Goofy, however, who is responsible (Gawsh!) for the chaos that Mickey strives valiantly against when all the orchestra's instruments are squashed flat by a falling elevator.

Poor Maestro Mouse! In spite of it all, he doggedly conducts the incredible array of noise that issues (and is broadcast to the nation on the radio) from these fragmented trombones and glockenspiels played (though that's not the right word) by the gang.

The drops of sweat fly from his brow. He knows he is presiding over a shambles, a catastrophic cacophony—but does he quit? Of course not! This man-mouse has guts. He has moral substance. No wonder he quickly became in the United States a hero-in-spite-of-himself.

But he became the kind of hero who was forced, by the need to maintain his reputation, to forsake some of the small mischiefs and misdemeanors of his youth. If he put a foot wrong, the Disney studios were flooded with protest mail. Mickey had become a national symbol, guardian of the fiber of the country. It was a mere six years from 1928 to 1934, when Cole Porter included in the musical *Anything Goes* a song called "You're the Top." This song is a brilliant procession of lines and rhymes, in which the "you" addressed is compared to every conceivable symbol of the very best—the Coliseum, the Louvre Museum, the leaning tower of Pisa, the smile on the Mona Lisa, and so on. And who should be at the climax of this array of flattering comparisons? You've got it:

"... a symphony by Strauss/You're a Bendel bonnet/A Shakespeare sonnet—/You're Mickey Mouse!"

For a cartoon character with an odd little voice, Mickey Mouse had a stunningly quick rise to "the Top." And since then, for very small persons of whatever age, he has never jumped down again. He is definitely someone to look—and talk—up to.
1994

Shawshank and a Supersonic Icon

I'd only seen the like of it on film before. But this was taking place on a rather chilly autumn day just outside Edinburgh. It wasn't a celluloid moment.

There were thousands of us in the audience. Some sat or stood on the roofs of cars and vans. Workmen had climbed up and perched all over an earth-moving machine. Hundreds were pressed up against the fence as if they simply HAD to get as near as they could. The rest of us just stood outside our cars. We had not been waiting very long. The event we were there to witness was timetabled.

And then—only a little later than scheduled—out of a nearly blue, faintly hazy sky, its characteristic roar increasing steadily as it made its descent toward the runway, Concorde appeared.

The famed supersonic passenger plane had been part of regular airport traffic in a select few cities with only one serious period of absence since January 1976. I had myself seen it on several occasions—on the tarmac at London's Heathrow and taking off; it was spellbinding when stationary. As it surged skywards en route to New York, it was a spine-shivery combination of magical elegance and raw power. It halved the conventional flight time of that transatlantic journey. From the ground you watched as it quite simply vanished into the sky as if, even at such a low altitude, it wanted to display its astonishing superiority to the usual expectations of time and space. Only far above the clouds though, did it travel like a bullet, at twice the speed of sound.

But today was billed as the decisive moment of this remarkable bird-fish-plane's final retirement from carrying passengers. Hearing on TV at breakfast that there was to be a specially designated viewing place from which to watch its last landing and take-off in the Scottish capital, how could I miss this occasion?

I thought there might be a small gathering of enthusiasts. Not at all. There were THOUSANDS. Line upon line of parked cars in a vast field. And as the plane came down, the stillness and concentration in that area by the runway, were palpable. In that sea of people, there wasn't a single head or eye that was not transfixed; children who had been running about were rooted to the spot. Everyone, held in a kind of frozen singleness of attention, was determined not to miss a split second of the experience. We were arrested.

This was not a film. But the closest to it I have seen was when the entire jail exercising in *The Shawshank Redemption* is rendered motionless and in awe as an old gramophone scratches out Mozart's "Che soave zeffiretto" from *The Marriage of Figaro* over the speaker system.

We talk glibly of unforgettable moments. Most of us remember exactly where we were and what we were doing when we first heard about certain earth-shattering events. Sometimes, however, such "defining" moments are not shattering at all—but elating. Man's first step on the lunar landscape, for instance.

Increasingly the ubiquitous media lay claim to unforgettable moments—the toppling of Saddam Hussein's statue, the time a lone and intrepid Chinese man refused to move out of the path of an oncoming tank. But such moments are still not direct experience, even when we watch them live. Later that day, back home, I watched on TV as the Concorde that had been in Edinburgh, and two other Concordes out of the entire extant fleet of seven, landed at London and slowly did a lap of honor. It was stirring. But what I will remember was the firsthand experience in Edinburgh a few hours earlier. It was not an experience that could or would be replayed until it loses all impact. It seems that there is a thirst, in spite of the impressive immediacy of TV reportage, to be there, on the spot.

I stood next to a Scot who, like me, had decided that morning to see Concorde's Last Stand. "I just happened to be in Edinburgh," he explained, "and I thought, why not? Look," he interrupted himself, "that could be it now!" There was a plane, not very distinguishable, moving in the very faded distance. But no; it was a boring, tubby kind of passenger plane and a distinct anti-climax. It trundled along the runway looking commonplace and clumsy. We ignored it. Then there was a small private plane taking off. And a courier plane, rotund and serviceable, weighted down with parcels. Then a middle-sized aircraft emblazoned with super graphics announcing that it belonged to one of the cut-price airlines that have been enormously increasing their market share in recent years. But still no Concorde.

When it finally showed up, the contrast between these everyday buses with wings that ply our airways and the supreme design of what we had actually come to see could hardly have been greater. It was weird. Concorde belongs to the 1950s and 60s; yet it still looks futuristic in 2003 compared with these far younger machines. I was struck by its leanness and length; by the finesse of its needle-sharp tail, its air-piercing nose. It did a carefully controlled "twirl" for us on the tarmac, and out of the flight deck window emerged a blue and white St. Andrew's flag. Then it stood for a while to let us savor our admiration. What could be more smoothly, gracefully, rightly designed? Yet we are told that its shape was entirely dictated by function; this was simply discovered to be what would work best for sound barrier-breaking flight. Concorde was not made to look beautiful. Nothing about it is cosmetic. It is an ultimate, engineered accolade for the philosophy of "form follows function."

It taxied off slowly toward the airport buildings in order to allow its passengers to disembark. Our collective moment of witness was over.

"Well," said my brief companion, "back to the real world." We both laughed, coming down to earth again with a bump.

I wondered: why do we relegate such brief wonder to "unreality?" And why have we—as too many people have averred with "realistic" mundaneness—now "seen the last" of such a bold, aspirational, imaginative breakthrough in air travel? How can these down-to-earthers be so VERY sure that it will now take six or seven hours from New York to London forever? That supersonic travel is over for good and all? Why should we believe this kind of music will never be played again? How dare we assume that what is inside heads and hearts can be so easily, so finally, so expediently extirpated?

As one of the prisoners in Shawshank said: "That's the beauty of music. They can't take that away from you."

2003

XII.
Making and Doing

If I Were Glueless, I'd Be Clueless

It was a bit odd. The staircase rose in all its 1900s self-importance. But it went nowhere. It just disappeared into the ceiling.

When we bought our new home from Queenie Leven, she suggested that we might contrive a unique decorative feature by balancing a tropical fish tank halfway up this surreal stairway. (We noticed, however, that she had never taken her own advice.) But I had boldly claimed there would be no problem removing the staircase.

Queenie's parents had divided this house in two sometime in the 1950s. It enabled them to sell the upper half as a separate domicile with its own outside stairs and a front door where a window had been. In this way, they could afford to stay in the lower half. But they had spent as little as possible on the conversion—thus the unremoved staircase.

The dismantling of the stairway quickly established itself as a priority. But I knew our neighbors owned its upper reaches rising from a small to a larger landing. If the lower stairs were taken away, how could I be sure the higher flights would not consequently disintegrate?

I could not be sure. But I am always impressed by others' advice when it agrees with my opinion, so I asked around and found some advice of that sort. And with such assurance, in a daring mood, I took hold of a crowbar, a wide chisel, and a claw hammer, and (with apologies to Marcel Duchamp) ascended the staircase—fully clothed—and set to work at the very top.

They knew how to make things properly in 1900. The first part was vigorously resistant to my prying and walloping. But at last it came away; then the rest of the staircase, in response to my ministrations, creaked and sprang apart, riser after tread after riser after tread until in no time the hall floor had a pile of large pine boards on it—and no staircase. This unexpected obligingness took me by surprise.

What impressed me above all, though, was the *construction* of the stairs. Only old-fashioned nails had been used, not one single screw—and (this filled me with the utmost admiration) not one dab or smear or hint of glue.

This artifact had been constructed, of course, in a period when "Do-It-Yourself" hadn't been invented. I'm sure the carpenter had undergone a rigorous apprenticeship and knew perfectly well that nails, straight and true, are more than adequate as a means for fixing together a staircase. By the time of my intervention, it had lasted 80 years without shift or twist and would presumably have lasted for centuries more. So well made was the staircase, in fact, that 20 years later, there's still no sign, I'm happy to report, of our upstairs neighbors plunging through our ceiling as they thunder up and down the portion of stairs left unto them.

One must also remember that the old carpenter lived well before the days of ubiquitous epoxy. Even as late as the 1950s, the only glue in our school carpentry shop was a stinking witch's brew that looked like toffee but was probably made of something like rabbit bones or powdered halibut. It had to be heated fiercely in a small iron pot before being usable. The brush to spread it was clogged into a thick unbending fist. It was enough to make you abandon any thought of becoming a cabinetmaker.

But today, we live in a wonderful world of glutinous, mucilaginous, gummy, and adhesive availability. How humans have advanced in their stickiness! Not just the ferociously fast super glues that hold anything together forever before you can say "Help!" but contact adhesives that flatly secure vast sheets, wood glues that claim to be stronger than the wood they fix, weather-resistant glues that bond anything from bricks to drainpipes—the list is endless.

And look at the advances in sticky-tape technology. Ordinary tape is itself a major revolution. Before that, to wrap a parcel in brown paper, the tape my mother used was itself a brown-paper strip with a gum one had to lick. It tasted unmentionable, and if you made it too wet, you washed away all traces of adhesiveness. Nor was it much good at going round corners.

Modern parcel tape has changed all that. You can now mummify a parcel in a few seconds so that it is impossible for the postal services or the recipient to open it. There is multipurpose duct tape; masking tape, and carpet tape, fabric tape, invisible tape, insulating tape—a glorious bewilderment of tapes.

The glues I like best are the kind that come in foot-long tubes and are applied with a gun. Few things are constructed around here these days without this glue.

If anyone down the line in, say, 2050, decides to take apart all the changes I have made to this house—the panels and walls, the boards and floors, the shelves and dividers—they will, I am sorry to say, have to deal with more than nails. They will have to deal with glue. Lashings and layerings and oozings and runnings and smearings and smudgings of glue.

Some brands of gun-glue, however, make claims that strike even this enthusiast as over the top. "NO MORE NAILS" they proclaim. "GRABS LIKE NAILS!" "GRIP IT!" "RAPID GRAB!" It is all very impressive, but there is still a lurking suspicion somewhere inside me. The advertising never says how *long* the glue lasts. But suppose it has a life span of only 60 years? Suppose everything I've glued begins to peel away, fall off, and drop down?

So, while I fire glue into every conceivable nook and cranny, I must confess I still use nails and screws, too, as insurance. Well—you know—*just in case.*

2001

Cowshed Door

Ah! The subtlety of it! How like a snake in the grass does *conventionality* creep up on you. But then perhaps unconventionality can also catch you unawares.

Take the new cowshed door, for instance.

Did you know that a cowshed door comes under the critical spotlight of societal expectations no less stringently than higher forms of life do—that some cowshed doors are considered normal and some are not? I certainly didn't, and I've just finished making one.

I asked Mr. Graveson, the weekly visiting grocer, what was wrong with it.

"It's an eyesore!" was his cheery pronouncement.

I asked Mr. Hodgson, the professional carpenter, who had supplied the timber.

After a pause to consider, he summed up his feelings by observing, "Well … it's just, let us say, rather *unusual.*"

The farmer's wife laughed at it openly.

The farmer, after shaking his head for a few moments in incredulous appreciation of my mistake, said, "Nay, lad! Never mind! *It stops t' 'ole!*"

It does that, all right. It needed to.

If there was one force bent on preventing me hanging the new door on its hinges, it was the Yorkshire wind. All the winds in the Northern Hemisphere rushed through that hole in the wall. Something decidedly solid was called for. And, now that the job is done, I haven't heard a single complaint from any of the cows inside. They are no longer frozen in their stalls, hocks shivering, moaning at the winter moon. Unquestionably the door "stops t' 'ole"; like a cork in a bottle. Though it sounds like boasting, I can claim without fear of contradiction, that this door is a perfect fit.

And that, in fact, is the problem.

The hole, you see, is not rectangular. Its corners aren't all square. "Trapezoidal" is possibly nearer to it. So, with enormous ingenuity, let me tell you, I fashioned my door to the precise but irregular geometry of this shape.

Now, as any devotee of Chinese puzzles will tell you, what goes in one way, won't go in another way. In other words, my custom-built cowshed door can only be hung one way round.

A door, when you think about it, is basically a strong timber framework with vertical boards nailed onto one side of it. All this I knew, and all this I did. And having done it—only after I had completely finished it—did the awful truth dawn. This door could only be hung—*inside out.*

There is little doubt about it. Its inside is outside, and its outside is inside. The approaching world can see its magnificent framework, its struts vertical, horizontal, and diagonal. This is the skeleton that should face inwards. But what the cows can see are the flat boards that ought to face outwards. The world—oh dire embarrassment!—can plainly see what convention dictates should be shyly secreted and politely hidden from the general view. Instead, pretension is shattered, custom disrupted, and good appearance flouted by immodest exposure.

But am I ashamed? Am I hanging my head? No, I am not. This, I have decided, is a new fashion in cowshed doors. After all, why should the finest intricacies of one's workmanship be forever concealed? Besides, as I mentioned, the cows are perfectly happy. They are untroubled. Not one of them has shown the slightest sign of being mooved by my unconventional door.

1975

In Our House, There Live a Scottish Woman and an English Man. Only One of Us Likes Porridge.

Our breakfast table groans under various species of muesli and cornflake, but is rarely asked to support a steaming bowl of porridge.

This may seem odd. After all, we live in Scotland where porridge is celebrated in verse and recipe as virtually a national dish. There are even rumors the Scots invented it. But although my wife is unquestionably Scottish, since childhood she has never liked porridge. Neither the taste of it nor the smell of it. On the other hand, I'm English and like the stuff.

I suppose we can't all be typical.

So if I find myself, as I now do, with a sudden sense of porridge deficiency, the decent thing to do is wait until she's left for work, and (since I work at home) indulge the whim once she's out of sniffing range. I've tried it for the past three winter mornings, and there have been no rumors yet of divorce proceedings.

I am even beginning to think that a day is not worthy of the name if it does not kick off with the warm comfort of porridge. It "sticks," they say, "to the ribs." I can vouch for it.

My liking for porridge, I should observe, is a remarkable example of the triumph of excellence over education.

I don't believe I had eaten any porridge at home before going away to boarding school. But I soon found that it was a favorite concoction of the school kitchen.

I suppose it was cheap. It also retains heat like a woolly blanket while being transported from kitchen to dining hall to feed a mass of ravenous boys. But, like some other school dishes, school porridge was not the edifying experience it ought to have been. It was lumpy. It formed a soggy crust. It was sticky or solid or both. It was, to borrow a splendid Scottish word, *gluddery*. I fancy that only Oliver Twist could possibly have wanted more of it. I realize now that it was a travesty of the real thing.

238

Of course, I was not at school in Scotland, or it would surely have been different. Here they treat oatmeal with a passion underscored by sands-of-time tradition, if not downright superstition. An articulate and funny Glasgow journalist named Clifford Hanley wrote that "outside Scotland, porridge is often a highly offensive experience" and that "alien races brutalize this magnificent Scots dish by heaving sugar over it; or syrup, or even jam. To the Scot, these practices have all the allure of eating anchovies with chocolate sauce."

But there are Scots who are much less strict and purist and at least allow children to sprinkle sugar on their porridge without any dire warning that this may irreparably damage their Scottishness. Robert Louis Stevenson no less, when he was a child, drew maps on his porridge with syrup trailing off his spoon. And I admit freely that although I put salt in my porridge as I cook it, *on* it I find the crunch and flavor of Demerara sugar (a light-brown sugar with large granules) utterly delicious.

What I do also greatly enjoy, though, and this is definitely a Scottish refinement, is having the piping porridge in one bowl and creamy milk, very cold, in another. You take a spoonful of porridge and submerge it in the milk before moving it to your mouth. The combination of hot and cold is delectable. If you pour milk directly into the porridge bowl, the milk grows sadly warm as you eat, and also it dilutes the porridge.

Fanatics (Scottish, naturally) maintain you should stir porridge with only one hand—I forget which—while it is cooking and that you should eat it with a horn spoon, standing up. You should stir it with a spurtle (a long wooden stirring stick that originated in Scotland). And use proper steel-cut oats. Rolled oats may cook faster, but they make true Scots tremble with horror.

And yet … quick-cooking oatmeal is made and marketed in Scotland, and I like it almost as much as properly-made porridge. But then I'm English, and I had my palate ruined by school food, so my opinion doesn't count.

I love the way the Scots have made this dish all their own. They would have us think that as spinach is to Popeye, so porridge is to gigantic muscular kilted highlanders tossing the caber.

Larousse, the authority on cuisine, paints a different picture, suggesting that porridge is an ancient Celtic dish, but may not have been a uniquely Scottish invention. It is eaten in Wales, Ireland, and throughout England, too.

I might add that both Goldilocks and the three not-very-gruntled bears had a famously soft spot for porridge, and there is no evidence that any of them had one soupçon of Scottish blood.

But Scotland is more identified with porridge than is any other country. In different areas, it even has different names, such as … "lite," "milgruel," "Tartan-purry," and "parritch."

And once a year The Golden Spurtle World Porridge Making Championship takes place in a small Scottish village called Carrbridge in Inverness-shire. Which seems entirely as it should be.

Authentic Scottish Porridge
(lumps optional)

This recipe is from *The Scots Kitchen* by F. Marian McNeill, first published in 1929, and still available from Mercat Press in Edinburgh. Note that the proportions are vague, unless you have "saltspoons" and "breakfastcup" measures at hand. Modern recipes call for two cups of water per cup of oats (serves three to four). While it doesn't say so explicitly, this recipe is undoubtedly for steel-cut oats—also known as "pinhead" oats, Irish or Scotch oatmeal, porridge oats, etc. (Note that it is not necessary to soak the oats overnight.) A line at the top of the recipe proclaims: "The One and Only Method."

Allow for each person:

One breakfastcupful of water
A handful of oatmeal (about an ounce and a quarter)
A small saltspoonful of salt

Use fresh spring water and be particular about the quality of the oatmeal. Midlothian oats are unsurpassed the world over.

Bring the water to the boil and as soon as it reaches boiling-point add the oatmeal, letting it fall in a steady rain from the left hand and stirring it briskly the while with the right, sunwise. … A porridge-stick, called a spurtle, and in some parts a theevil, or, as in Shetland, a gruel-tree, is used for this purpose.

Be careful to avoid lumps, unless the children clamour for them. When the porridge is boiling steadily, draw the mixture to the side and put on the lid. Let it cook for from 20 to 30 minutes according to the quality of the oatmeal, and do not add the salt, which has a tendency to harden the meal and prevent its swelling, until it has cooked for at least 10 minutes. On the other hand, never cook porridge without salt.

Ladle straight into porringers or soup-plates and serve with small individual bowls of cream, or milk, or buttermilk. Each spoonful of porridge, which should be very hot, is dipped in the cream or milk, which should be quite cold, before it is conveyed to the mouth.

2003

The Wisdom of Mr. Percy the Plumber

On a morning like this morning, I think I am quite justified in feeling that this is the kind of place that is no longer thought to exist. To be able to sit comfortably astride a Yorkshire stone wall in March and feel the sun-warmth and gaze from the surrounding greenness up at the white wonderland of the snow hills, wisped with cloud and lazed over by meandering, stretched shadows—just to sit and see and listen: this is being conscious!

People in impatient cities long for this kind of quietness—which makes me admit that Mr. Eddie Percy, local plumber, *does* know a thing or two.

Of course, plumbers anywhere (in England) take a very long time to come and do things for you. An *emergency* is another matter; but a non-urgent job like fitting a pump to increase the force of your bathwater to something more than a slow trickle—well, as Mr. Percy remarked, with a chuckle, to Mrs. McRae, "That Christopher 'as to learn that when you live in the country, you 'ave to be a bit patient, like."

Mr. Percy is the epitome of plumbers. A frantically burst pipe he will put right instantly. An inessential water pump he will take a good three years to install.... What's the hurry?

A year and two months after I ordered it, Eddie managed to get hold of a pump for me. I bought it and asked him to come and put it in. "Aye, I'll fit you in," he said absently, and then: "Eh! I 'eard a good 'un t' other day about yon farmer-chap lives up near you at High Rigg!" And he launched into the four hundred and twenty-second funny story he'd told me that year.

I have come to know Eddie pretty well. Anyone who had chatted with him once or twice a week for at least eighteen months would. Each time, he used a comic red herring to fob me off. "Aye! I'll fit you in!" he'd add—but he never did.

Then one day, I asked Miss Rawsthorne, his longtime secretary, why it was I couldn't persuade him to come and fit the pump. She gave me a look. She said, "You mustn't *smile*. If you smile, he thinks you don't mean it."

I could hear Eddie regaling someone at the far end of his yard, in the hut where he cut, with magical skill, large sheets of window glass. As I walked down the yard, wanting to laugh and smile more than ever, I reigned in my risible tendencies by an act of sheer determination. Miss R was right. Completely without smiling, I asked him straight out to come and fit the pump *tomorrow*. He looked surprised, baffled by my change of character perhaps. "Oh," he said, "you're in a right 'urry, then?" No funny stories this time. Next day, at 8.30 a.m., his men were knocking on my front door.

But Eddie knows a thing or two. Patience is the prime and necessary virtue in the country. If you don't have it, you don't fit in. And smiling is humanity's greatest symbol of patience....

On a morning like this, so utterly still, wide and clear in the universal sun, these unchanging fields and farms and rising hills seem to be patience itself—patience, as Shakespeare has it, smiling. Sitting on the lichen-powdered rocks of this wall, it is easy to feel a monumental gladness that a hurried man can still find a place—outside or inside him—where exigency is reduced to virtually no importance at all and such trivial anxieties as, for example, the time it takes for his bath water to run, fade away....

The pump, now fitted, turned out not to be powerful enough to have any effect upstairs in the house. I phoned Eddie sternly and immediately. He did have a secondhand pump that was bigger, as it happened. I drove to his yard to get it—to save time. Breathlessly, the workmen installed it before lunch. The water surged vigorously through the alarmed pipes....

But Eddie knew a thing or two....

Some days I can walk over these fields, anxious, preoccupied, confusedly oblivious to the tranquil generosity of this unbelievable landscape. I am enveloped in the noise of myself, spoiling the gentleness of things, pushed and pulled by pressures to achieve—to do things now, if not yesterday. But this morning, I am in keeping with the staying, calming quality of it all. A deep silence of spirit has hold of me, and I can listen and hear. A cow up at Ken's farm coughs. A goose at Percival's, by the bridge, honks distantly. A sheep— no, two sheep—bleat somewhere over by the disused quarry. Down by the trees—the chestnut and the line of ashes—the beck flows, and a springtime conglomeration of hungry birds is chattering and muttering and exulting. A single bird nearby clarions cheekily.... A soft roar of Saturday traffic on the road to the Lakes seems to come from miles away, and then, quite suddenly, with a rushing sound and a muted clatter contained by the surrounding slopes, a two-carriage train charges straight through the valley. Strange to consider that this hardly-used railway line was once the most strident evidence in the area of industrialized man's impatience, disrupting the peace and beauty of the countryside. Today, it seems completely apt, a suitable part of everything, contributing to the rural tranquility....

But this cannot be said of my new water pump. Not only does it leak. Not only have I spent another nine months trying to get Mr. Percy to repair it. Not only is my bath filled to overflowing before I expect it. But also—THE WRETCHED THING MAKES AN INCREDIBLE RACKET!

I can't blame this on Eddie's rush to install it. I can't say he didn't hint and imply and suggest, in true plumberial fashion, that a pump might not be an entirely sound idea. I can hardly complain that he bludgeoned me into buying it.

All I can say is that I should never have stopped smiling.

But out here, this morning, there is smiling. In this sun-filled space and openness rests a sense of—well, a sense of proportion. There may be crises, and there may be governments incoming and outgoing, and coal slowdowns, and oil shortages, and electricity cuts, and train drivers' disputes—yet a man can still somehow, somewhere, experience this expansive reach of stillness....

And I have unplugged my pump.
1974

Up the Chimney, Please

Smoke, as the song says, gets in your eyes—though it seems to me that eyes are by no means the only place smoke gets in. Some friends tell me that every time they light their living room fire, their bathroom fills with smoke. I have informed them, out of the bottomless depths of my own experience, that this is no mystery to me. Smoke is more than ingenious. It can get, as the farmer said of the lawyer, where water can't.

One of the determined drives of my life in the last few years has been a concentrated effort to make the smoke in our house travel precisely, and only, in the direction mapped out for it—i.e. up the chimney. Anyone who thinks this is a facile and trivial matter hasn't tried it. It is, or should be, a truism that mankind may have examined Mars at close quarters, but still doesn't know how to cope with an awkward downdraft in a common domestic flue pipe.

Things would be comparatively easy, really, if the primitive desire for an *open* fire wasn't so compelling. Our potbellied stove is so completely enclosed that its smoke has no possible escape but up and out. But the fire inside it is invisible.

I've never been greatly persuaded that one's life divides into neat periods. Blue and pink periods in reality run into each other blurrily. "Pre" and "post" suggest a linear time sequence that doesn't successfully describe *continuance.* All the same, new perceptions do intrude upon an expanding sphere of awareness, and looking at my own paintings I shouldn't perhaps be too surprised that certain kinds of billowing movement and a tendency to search for hazy tones that wreathe, and a fondness for forms that uncurl, have shown up without my quite knowing how.

I do, however, know *why.*

The reason is my involvement in the ancient art of open fireplace building. An illustration of how *closely* involved I am occurred a couple of days ago when someone phoned me only to be told I would have to call him back. When I did, my caller asked: "Were you really 'up the chimney' as whoever-it-was-who-answered the-phone said you were?" I had to admit it was the unvarnished truth. I should have added that it is not, in fact, one of my favorite places of residence. It is exceptionally dusty and exceptionally confined. It makes me think of *Mary Poppins* or Charles Kingsley's *Water Babies*.

The whole purpose of making our open fireplace is aesthetic rather than purely practical. We already have, in the same room, as aforementioned, the ferociously effective, closed-in potbellied stove. This black cast iron globe that looks rather like an ancient bomb is the source of untold heat. We sometimes have to retire to remote corners of the room or even other parts of the house to avoid meltdown. But the open fireplace is for seeing rather than feeling. It is for welcome, and for a sense of history, and for the sweet smell of wood ash, and for orange uplicking flames to gaze into, and for slowly fading embers. We want it because we haven't got it. Anyone whose childhood was centrally heated conceives a longing for living and visible fire, and even those of us who were not reared on radiators, relish burning, glowing, crackling logs.

Actually, this fireplace is really Frank's rather than mine.

Frank is the retired farmer who has in one way or another rebuilt most of our house. I am his laborer. I helped him lift the stone lintel, broken in three when it was removed thirty years ago from the same approximate position in the wall and since then ignominiously used in the foundation of a Nissen hut. We heaved it onto an iron rail, and then Frank did an invisible mending job on the fragments, and it now looks like new. Well, not *new* exactly. Really it looks like *old*—which, of course, is just what it is meant to look like.

Frank did a marvelous job of reconstruction. He quarried out of the brick-botched wall a wonderful stone fireplace, nooked and crannied. He angled a narrowing chimney inside the wall to tunnel the smoke up to the existing flue pipe. He uncovered an oak beam and plastered the wall between it and the lintel below it. He welded together an elaborate iron grate and a device that I still don't know how to spell—phonetically it is a "wreckin." It is a swinging arm to hold a cooking pan just above the fire.

Then came the day of the Great Lighting.

The flames leaped and danced upward, and the smoke poured and pouted and puffed and rushed … into the room.

The ratio of downdraft to updraft was about 100 to 1. Chokingly bemused, I stood it for a while. Then I opened the window. Then I went into the next room. Then I went into the garden. Not so Frank. He sat, enveloped in smoke, on the stone shelf to the left of his fireplace. And he gazed up the chimney with unutterable gloom—though in Frank's case, gloom tends to be extremely utterable. Under whatever breath he had left on this occasion (and most of it must have been smoke), he proceeded to let out a slow, deliberate, intense train of—well, of undeleted expletives. To the uninitiated, this growl of carefully orchestrated verbal fury might seem at least arresting. But I knew, through experience, that it signified nothing but a richly ironic sense of humor.

After this, came weeks and months of Trying to Solve the Problem of the Fireplace. Frank's wife said he sat at home in the evenings, brooding. She didn't need to ask him for his thoughts. She knew he was planning some new move. Suddenly he would leap up and thrust his head enquiringly up their chimney, anxious for inspiration, oblivious to the flames singeing his back hair.

Come morning, he would arrive at our place once more, with a freshly constructed canopy, or firebricks to bring in the sides, or a new length of asbestos flue pipe, or a deeper grate. Pyromania seized hold of both of us. Fire after fire was lit. And very gradually, we started to outwit the recalcitrant smoke.

A possible source of unwanted air upstairs was walled in. Cracks in the skirting boards were filled. The chimney pot was removed. Then it was replaced by first one spinning cowl and then another—a story in itself. The final shape of the fireplace canopy was settled, and the old refrigerator sides (of which Frank had made it) were covered with stone. This time of experiment, despair, sudden hope, and partial triumph was a time when the house smelled permanently of burning newspaper and charcoaled wood, and a blue mist hung delicately in its atmosphere.

We use the fire in the summer to counteract an evening's chill. Sometimes it burns like a dream. It looks good, and it feels good. But with a change of wind or a sudden lull, wisps of subtle, insinuating vapor start to slide under the canopy and waft weightlessly into the room. By 10:30, the far walls are becoming strangely indistinguishable, eyes are smarting, and the animals all wander sleepily upstairs in search of clearer zones.

Frank's Fireplace still remains to some degree Frank's Problem. And I am not entirely sure he is unhappy about this. Some people like a persistent challenge. They *like* to be able to say (in a growl, under their breath), "Well, we haven't been beaten *yet*."

1978

As noted at the beginning of this book, it is © 2004 by Christopher Andreae. All essays in this book except "Shawshank and a Supersonic Icon" originally appeared in The Christian Science Monitor. These essays have been revised and/or retitled for this book by the author with the Monitor's permission. As detailed below, individual essays are either © Christopher Andreae (© C.A.), or © The Christian Science Monitor (© CSM).

"Of Whiskers and Old Socks" (p13-15) CSM July 2 '01 as "Yet Another Product of Bad Behavior" © CSM / "A Time to Exuberate Rumbustiously" (p16-18) CSM Aug 20 '92 as "A Rumbustious Writer's Defining Moment" © CSM / "Danger: Booksellers at Work" (p19-22) CSM Oct 2 '96 as "Firsthand Experience, Secondhand Books" © CSM / "In the Library, With a Book" (p23-27) CSM Oct 21 '92 as "The Abode of the Book Lover and His Treasures" © CSM / "Spot, Domino and the Emmas" (p31-34) CSM Aug 14 '93 as "A Lap Full of Spots" © CSM / "The Sleeping-Dog Factor" (p35-37) CSM May 24 '84 as "The Sleeping-Dog Factor" © C.A. / "It's a Bird! It's a Plane! It's a Dog!" (p38-40) CSM Jun 5 '84 as "It's a Bird! It's a Plane! It's a Dog!" © C.A. / "Dodge the Puppy, Olé" (p41-43) CSM May 28 '97 as "Exercising a New Puppy to Imagined Cries of Olé" © CSM / "Unqualified Cat" (p47-49) CSM Jun 11 '80 as "Everthankful Purrs" © C.A. / "The Mouse Question" (p50-54) CSM Aug 12 '92 as "The Mouse Question" © CSM / "Think Butterfly" (p55-57) CSM Jan 4 '02 as "Butterfly Thoughts Transport Me" © CSM / "Hoots, Mon!" (p58-60) CSM Mar 19 '03 as "Compared to TV, Real Life Is a Hoot" © C.A. / "City Fox" (p61-64) CSM May 28 '91 as "The Streetwise Cousin of the Cautious Country Fox" © C.A. / "New Pets" (p65-67) / Dec 4 '02 as "Not Every Pet Is Warm and Fuzzy" © C.A. / "A Serious Parade" (p71-73) CSM Aug 28 '80 as "A Laughable Parade" © C.A. / "My Dry-Stone Wall" (p74-77) CSM Jan 12 '72 as "Something That Does Love a Wall" © C.A. / "Hercules Part 1" (p78-80) CSM May 18 '78 as "How Hercules Found a New Purpose" © C.A. / "Hercules Part 2" (p81-83) CSM Oct 19 '78 as "And You Call Yourself a Shepherd" © C.A. / "The Great Midnight Milk Run" (p84-88) CSM Jan 18 '90 as "The Great Midnight Milk Run © CSM / "Departing Delight (p89-90) CSM Sep 14 '94 as (part of) "Glimmers of Delight" © CSM / "An American in Edinburgh" (p93-95) CSM Sep 9 '96 as "A Quiet American Turns Out Not to Be" © CSM / "Someone's Got to Cha-Cha" (p96-99) CSM Dec 31 '86 as "Someone's Got to Cha-Cha" © C.A. / "Live Ringers" (p100-102) CSM Feb 23 '88 as "Tales from a Bell Tower" © C.A. / "A Matter of Resolve" (p103-104) CSM Jan 4 '95 as "Twiddling Thumbs Over New Year's Resolutions" © CSM / "Oh Wad Some Power . . . the Giftie Gie Us" (p105-108) CSM Sep 4 '87 as "Oh Wad Some …; … the Giftie Gie Us" © C.A. / "Dreams of Glorious Orbitation" (p109-111) CSM Dec 10 '85 as "Dreams of Glorious Orbitation" © C.A. / "Don't Bank on It" (p112-114) CSM May 19 '88 as "Laughing All the Way to the Bank" ©

C.A. / "Columns in Mercurial Moonlight" (p115-117) CSM Feb 6 '92 as "Columns in Mercurial Moonlight" © CSM / "Hand It to Her Majesty" (p121-123) CSM May 30 '96 as "The Royal Ruckus Over Her Majesty's Dreadful Digits" © CSM / "Sir Alec Is Everywhere" (p124-126) CSM Nov 20 '96 as "That Famous Face, So Often Unseen" © CSM / "Boulez in a Taxi" (p127-130) CSM Sep 10 '98 as "The Maestro's Movable Performance" © CSM / "Maestro" (p131-133) CSM Dec 18 '85 as "Maestro" © C.A. / "Slow-Time Kid" (p137-138) CSM Nov 4 '81 as "The Genius of Slow Time" © C.A. / "Wake Up, You!" (p139-140) CSM Feb 24 '75 as "Techniques for Getting-Up-in-the-Morning" © C.A. / "Help!" (p141-143) CSM Sep 8 '97 as "Help, as Defined by Dogs and Children" © CSM / "You Might Have Warned Me, Miss Austen" (p144-145) CSM Jan 25 '77 as "Why Didn't You Warn Me, Miss Austen" © C.A. / "The Ultimate Parent?" (p146-149) CSM May 15 '79 as "The Make-or-Break Test" © C.A. / "Snowfields" (p150-152) CSM Feb 6 '03 as "Once Accelerated, Now Exhilarated by Fields" © C.A./ "Dawdling on the Way" (p155-157) CSM Feb 6 '02 as "Generations of Dawdling to School" © CSM / "The Blue Moon Awards" (p158-159) CSM Feb 15 '89 as "Is There a Blue Moon in the Sky Today?" © C.A. / "Such Glad Sweetness" (p160-162) CSM Oct 18 '02 as "During My Childhood, Life Was … Sweets" © C.A. / "The Taylor" (p163-165) CSM Oct 26 '98 as "His Words Still Shape My Own" © CSM / "The Herrick Event" (p166-169) CSM Jan 2 '85 as "Gather Ye Rose-Buds While Ye May—But Not With Me" © C.A. / "Asparagus and Other Flights of Fancy" (p173-175) CSM Apr 23 '98 as "Asparagus and Other Flights of Fancy" © CSM / "The Meaning of Gardens" (p176-79) CSM Aug 24 '76 as "A Search for the Meaning of Gardens" © C.A. / "Summer Can Start Now" (p180-182) CSM Jun 27 '03 as "The Heralds of Summer: Mini Stars and Maureen" © C.A. / "Gifts . . . and Gifts" (p183-184) CSM Jun 23 '99 as "Modern-Day Sharing Croppers" © CSM / "On Not Giving Up Supermarkets Just Yet" (p185-187) CSM Aug 11 '99 as "Neil's Bag of Tricks" © CSM / "Lord Northcliffe and the Thin Fireman" (p191-193) CSM Nov 2 '87 as "Extra! Extra! … and Less" © C.A. / "Seashells on a Plate" (p194-196) CSM Jul 2 '80 as "Carrying It Off" © C.A. / "A Little Light Praise" (p197-199) CSM Jan 15 '03 as "Let Us Now Praise Unfamous Men" © C.A. / "My Heart Is Merry and Bright—It's December 28" (p200-202) CSM Dec 28 '90 as "Those Festive Lights" © CSM / "Hearts to You" (p203-206) CSM Feb 14 '94 as "Hearts to You" © CSM / "Potter Cried 'Bosh!'" (p209-212) CSM Aug 7 '90 as "From the Pen Of Beatrix Potter" © CSM / "Legible Characters" (p213-215) CSM Jul 12 '02 as "If Not Legibly, Then With Character.…" © C.A. / "To Be Outwardly Inward" (p216-217) CSM Sep 19 '79 as "To Be Outwardly Inward" © C.A. / "Lot Number 179" (p218-222) CSM Jul 5 '90 as "The Subtle Theatrics of Bidding at Auctions" © CSM / "The Mouse for All Seasons" (p223-226) CSM Apr 27 '94 as "M-I-C-K-E-Y: The Mouse-Man for All Seasons" © CSM / "Shawshank and a Supersonic Icon" (p227-229) © C.A. / "If I Were Glueless, I'd Be Clueless" (p233-235) CSM Jun 4 '01 as "If I Were Glueless, I'd Be Clueless" © CSM / "Cowshed Door" (p236-237) CSM Mar 14 '75 as "From the

Cow's Viewpoint" © C.A. / "In Our House, There Live a Scottish Woman and an English Man; But Only One of Us Likes Porridge" (p238-241) CSM Feb 24 '03 as "A Zealous Convert in the Land of Oatmeal" © C.A. / "The Wisdom of Mr. Percy the Plumber" (p242-244) CSM May 1 '74 as "On the Wisdom of Plumbers" © C.A. / "Up the Chimney, Please" (p245-247) CSM Dec 13 '78 as "Up the Chimney" © C.A.

Printed in the United States
21803LVS00002B/274-285